The Scrolls and Christianity

Other volumes in this series:

THEOLOGICAL COLLECTIONS

II

THE SCROLLS AND CHRISTIANITY

Historical and Theological Significance

W. F. Albright
C. S. Mann
R. K. Harrison
Raymond E. Brown
John Pryke
Charles H. H. Scobie
F. F. Bruce
Max Wilcox
Matthew Black

Edited and
with an Introduction
and concluding chapter by
Matthew Black

LONDON

S·P·C·K

1969

First published in 1969
by S.P.C.K.
Holy Trinity Church
Marylebone Road
London N.W.1

Printed in Great Britain by
The Talbot Press (S.P.C.K.),
Saffron Walden, Essex

SBN 281 02288 7

CONTENTS

ABBREVIATIONS

I QpHab.	Habakkuk Commentary
I QS	Rule of the Community (Manual of Discipline)
I QSa (= I Q28a)	Rule of the Community (Appendix)
I QSb (= I Q28b)	Collection of Benedictions
I QM	War of the Sons of Light against the Sons of Darkness
I QH	Hymns of Thanksgiving
CD	Fragments of a Zadokite Work (Damascus Document)
IV Q Patr.	Patriarchal Blessings
IV Q Test.	Testimonia
IV Q Flor.	Florilegium
IV QpNah.	Nahum Midrash
IV QpPs. 37	Midrash on Psalm 37
IV QSl	Angelic Liturgy
IV Q Mess. ar.	Aramaic Messianic text (ed. J. Starcky, Mémorial Cinquantenaire de l'École des langues anciennes de l'Institut Catholique de Paris (1964), pp. 51-6)
Gen. Apoc.	Genesis Apocryphon

INTRODUCTION

Fewer and fewer doubts are being expressed nowadays about the identity of the sect of the Dead Sea Scrolls or the *terminus ad quem* for the deposit of the scrolls in the Caves (and, therefore, the date of the latest documents discovered at or near Qumran). Philological evidence, for instance, "forces the identification of the community at Qumran with the Essenes"[1] and "it is now probable that the oldest Qumran manuscripts date back to the early third century B.C. At the opposite end of the scale we have a fixed *terminus ad quem* at Masada, where numerous inscribed fragments have been found, some quite early, but none later than A.D. 73, when the fortress was stormed by the Romans".[2] In the light of Dr Albright's survey of the archaeological and palaeographical evidence "it is perfectly clear that the latest proposal for a different solution by a scholar of standing—G. R. Driver in his *The Judaean Scrolls: The Problem and a Solution* (Oxford, 1965)—has failed completely".[3]

These now firm conclusions give the Qumran documents a unique place and importance in the history of Biblical discovery; for they represent the remains (sometimes alas! only the debris) of a Jewish sectarian library from the time of Christ. The leather or parchment scrolls vary from complete scrolls, like the two now famous Isaiah scrolls, to merest fragments with little more than a single letter on them. They are mainly biblical writings, or biblically orientated writings: most of the Books of the Hebrew canon are represented, with, in addition, Hebrew and Aramaic fragments of the inter-testamental Apocrypha and Pseudepigrapha (Enoch, Jubilees, Tobit, the Testaments of the Twelve Patriarchs, etc.) and similar writings. A copper scroll, containing what appears to be an inventory of Temple treasure, is one of the most enigmatic of the finds.

The biblical manuscripts are of very great importance for the student of the Old Testament. Our earliest extant Hebrew manuscripts come from the tenth century A.D.: the biblical scrolls antedate these manuscripts by as much as ten centuries, yet the remarkable fact is that the text of the Old Testament is substantially the same text in A.D. 1000 as in A.D. 1. There are differences, of course, but these do not amount to any more or less than the kind of differences one finds between, say, the Vulgate translation and the

---

[1] Albright, below, p. 11   [2] Ibid., p. 15   [3] Below, p. 15

Hebrew Old Testament and the translation of the Hebrew in the Greek Old Testament, the so-called Septuagint. These biblical scrolls, in other words, are a remarkable testimony to the integrity of the Hebrew text and to the fidelity and care with which the Bible has been preserved down the centuries. Sir Frederick Kenyon is reported to have said in 1939: "There is indeed no probability that we shall ever find manuscripts of the Hebrew text going back to a period before the formation of the text which we know as Massoretic". Sir Frederick lived to see his word disproved in 1947, for these Qumran discoveries have, in fact, penetrated the Massoretic barrier, as it were, and enable us to form an idea of the nature of the Hebrew text in the early centuries of our era—in some cases undoubtedly the pre-Christian Hebrew text.[4]

The most important of these texts for the reconstruction of the history and beliefs of the Qumran sect—the main concern of the present collection of essays—are without doubt the non-biblical texts. (They can hardly be called secular or profane for they all deal with sacred subjects.) The commentaries were written so that the reader should read between the lines and draw comfort and strength, especially in times of persecution, from the writer's reflection on the events of his time, and in particular on the impending Day of Judgement which would right all Israel's wrongs on earth (Israel in this case being identified with the Qumran sectarians). These commentaries also provide the scholar with invaluable insights especially into the history of this sectarian movement. The *Manual of Discipline*, as its name implies, gives us some idea of the rules and organization of the sect but it is a miscellaneous collection (it closes with a Hymn or Song of Thanksgiving) and it also contains a long formal section summarizing the doctrine or theology of the Qumran sectarians, a section which is invaluable to the theologian. The same kind of value, historical and theological, attaches to the other documents, the *War Scroll*, and especially to the *Hodayoth* or *Hymns of Thanksgiving*, where indeed we receive most of our illumination about the doctrines and beliefs of Qumran.

These *Hodayoth* are not concerned with the systematic exposition of doctrine. Any doctrine that they contain is implicit and nowhere given in a single direct and comprehensive statement; like so much in the New Testament itself, however, it underlies the text and is easily discernible. The summary of the sect's doctrine in the *Manual of Discipline*, moreover, provides us with a valuable check on the doctrinal implications of the Thanksgiving scroll, and enables us to detect clear lines of crystallizing belief which bear a

[4] Cf. John Allegro, *The Dead Sea Scrolls, a Reappraisal* (Pelican, 1964), p. 59.

very marked resemblance to New Testament doctrine and which clearly have some historical connection with the New Testament.[5]

The present collection of essays seeks to present the scholars' verdicts, up to date, on the main problems raised by the scrolls, with special reference to their value as new evidence bearing on the types of Judaism current in Palestine in the New Testament period. The emphasis of the collection is more on the contribution of the scrolls to New Testament problems; nothing is included which deals directly with the fascinating and important question of the text of the Hebrew Bible. Naturally the first problem to be tackled is that of date and identity of the sect, a problem calling for an expert assessment of the archaeological, palaeographical, and historical evidence. This has been done by one of the foremost living authorities on the subject, Professor W. F. Albright, in collaboration with Dr C. S. Mann. The collection then goes on to a series of topics central in scroll research; and we have been fortunate in obtaining the services of two notable scholars in this field of study, Professor F. F. Bruce and Professor R. E. Brown, to deal respectively with the problem of Jesus, the Gospel and the Scrolls, and the messianism of the Qumran sect. Dr Harrison is well-known for his contributions to the archaeology of the Old Testament and Professor Scobie has recently written an important monograph on John the Baptist. Mr Pryke has made a special study of the subject on which he writes and Dr Wilcox is an authority on the Semitic background of the New Testament. I have been responsible for the concluding essay on "The Scrolls and Christian Origins"; this is not in any way intended as a summary or assessment of the other essays, though naturally account is taken of some of the views expressed; it is an attempt to state in general terms the position on this crucial issue which a wide consensus of scholars would now be prepared to accept.

The views expressed in each essay are those of the individual authors, who are solely responsible for them. There is also occasionally an overlapping of topics, but this is inevitable in such a collection. The attempt has been made throughout to express the frequently complex and confused issues in as simple and clear a way as possible. If the issues may seem to the expert occasionally to be over-simplified, the general reader can be assured that the essays nowhere contain distorted or tendentious theories.[6]

5 The English translation of G. Vermes (*The Dead Sea Scrolls in English*, Pelican Books, 1962) is recommended.

6 The most up-to-date "inventory" of editions of the scrolls is that of J. A. Sanders, *Palestinian Manuscripts*, 1947-67, in *Journal of Biblical Literature*, Vol. lxxxvi, Part IV, pp. 431ff. The more important bibliographies are also listed.

Abbreviations for the scrolls are the standard sigla and are listed on p. 6 above. The index has been prepared by the Rev. E. R. Ohannes, and Miss Mary C. Blackwood, with the assistance of Miss Patricia A. Mackie, all of St Mary's College.

St Mary's College
St Andrews MATTHEW BLACK

NOTES ON CONTRIBUTORS

The Reverend Dr Matthew Black is Principal of St Mary's College and Professor of Biblical Criticism in the University of St Andrews.

W. F. Albright is Professor Emeritus of Semitic Languages at Johns Hopkins University, Baltimore, Maryland.

The Reverend Dr C. S. Mann is Fellow in the Department of Near Eastern Studies at Johns Hopkins University, Baltimore, Maryland.

The Reverend Dr R. K. Harrison is Professor of Old Testament at Wycliffe College in the University of Toronto.

The Reverend Raymond E. Brown is a Roman Catholic priest of the Society of St Sulpice and Professor of Sacred Scripture at St Mary's Seminary, Roland Park, Baltimore, Maryland.

The Reverend John Pryke is Senior Lecturer in Divinity and Assistant Chaplain at the College of St Mark and St John, Chelsea.

The Reverend Dr Charles H. H. Scobie is Professor of New Testament Literature and Exegesis in the Presbyterian College, Montreal.

Dr F. F. Bruce is Rylands Professor of Biblical Criticism and Exegesis in the University of Manchester.

The Reverend Dr Max Wilcox is Reader and Head of the Department of Religious Studies in the University of Newcastle-upon-Tyne.

I

QUMRAN AND THE ESSENES: GEOGRAPHY, CHRONOLOGY, AND IDENTIFICATION OF THE SECT

W. F. ALBRIGHT AND C. S. MANN

I

NEITHER excavation nor philology is independently capable of providing a firm solution of the problem of the Essene sect of Judaism. Our available sources from Qumran do not mention the Essenes as such, and this apparent anomaly has given rise to every conceivable kind of hypothesis concerning the relation of the Essenes and the Qumran remains. However, our philological sources do provide significant material which, when properly evaluated, forces the identification of the community at Qumran with the Essenes.[1]

With varying degrees of detail and emphasis the Essenes are mentioned by Philo, Pliny, Josephus, Hippolytus, Solinus, Eusebius, and Epiphanius among others. Pliny and Solinus are our most important sources for the geographical location of the outstanding Essene community on the shores of the Dead Sea. The Latin text of Pliny (ob. A.D. 79) is commonly held to have been derived from information provided by the bibliophile and author Juba of Mauretania (fl. just before and after the Christian era), who wrote in Greek. There would seem to be no doubt that Pliny's source was originally Greek, for Solinus gives some of the material in a divergent Latin version, which can only be explained as coming from an independent translation. It is curious that this fact seems to have gone unnoticed hitherto, but it is perfectly plain to anyone accustomed to dealing with comparative translation (cf. Pliny, *Historia Naturalis*, v. 73, Solinus, *Collectanea Rerum Memorabilium*, xxv. 9. 12, and also Ch. Burchard, "Solin et les Esséniens: Remarques à propos d'une source négligée" (*Rev. Bib.* 64. 392-407, 1967), who very nearly grasps the point (p. 406).

Unfortunately, the most important passage in Pliny for the geographical location of the Essene community on the western shore of the Dead Sea is textually defective. This may be gathered from the fact that classical scholars have abandoned all attempts at literal translation, and have produced intrinsically absurd translations. For example, H. Rackham's version in the *Loeb Classical Library* has: "On the west side of the Dead Sea, and out of range of the noxious exhalations of the coast, is the tribe of the Essenes". To this passage there is no precise equivalent in Solinus, but his text does offer us the following: " . . . the Essenes (who) inhabit the west . . . retire from the ordinary usages of all peoples . . .". In spite of the defective text of Solinus, it is nevertheless a clarification of the equally defective text of Pliny. A reconstructed text of Pliny could read as follows:

Ab occident*ali* litore Esseni fugiunt usque *adhuc ea* quae nocent.[2]
On the western shore the Essenes avoid until *now those things* that are harmful.

The suggested completion of the text (indicated by italics) offers no radical re-writing of it, though it does assume two haplographies, while the construction *usque adhuc* (until now) was used from Plautus and Terence to the Latin Fathers. Without entering into further details about the text, it must be said that there is no evidence for placing the Essenes at a distance from the shores of the Dead Sea. Since both Pliny and Solinus, with slightly varying renderings of the original Greek, place the Essene settlement above Engedi, this can only mean (as has been pointed out by many scholars) going south down the Jordan-Dead Sea valley. Even if this interpretation of the Latin *infra* as meaning "south" should be wrong, it is still a fact that no other remotely comparable oasis between Jericho and Masada, and north of Engedi, can be found to accommodate the Essene community than that which housed the settlement of Qumran.

The excavations of R. de Vaux in the oasis formed by the waters of 'Ain Feshkha and two smaller springs have made it certain that the area was occupied at the same time as the monastery at Qumran. Equally, it has long been known that the level of the Dead Sea is now much higher than it was in Roman times, and the sonar soundings of Ralph Baney in 1960, north and south of Qumran, disclosed remains of stone constructions of some kind under the water, extending about 1½ miles from the present shore-line to where the shelf drops abruptly to a depth of over 300 feet.[3] From the shore to the edge of the under-water shelf there is a descent of some 50 feet, the caves near 'Ain Feshkha being now a half-mile from the shore-line. The Roman shore-line was then about one-and-a-half miles east of the present shore-line of the oasis. It is probable that the marshes now extending for over two miles along the shore between Qumran and 'Ain Feshkha were dry at that time, since the Dead Sea level was so much lower. In this case the irrigable area of the oasis was several times as extensive as it is today. There may well have been an additional number of small springs. In ancient times there were incomparably more palm trees than there are today, as shown by Baney's discovery under the Dead Sea, near Qumran, of partly fossilized palm trunks covered with layers of gypsum, calcite, and aragonite. In short, the lost Greek source which Pliny reproduced with his (*gens*) *socia palmarum* and Solinus by *palmis victitant* was entirely correct; the Essene community at Qumran indeed depended largely on groves of date palms for both companionship and nourishment.

2

From 1951 to 1955 R. de Vaux carried out excavations at the community centre in Qumran, which was the nearest inhabited site to Cave I, where the original finds of the scrolls were made.[4] In 1956 the excavations were extended to the cemetery, and in 1958 to the 'Ain Feshkha area. The excavations were conducted with exemplary care, and thanks to the evidence of successive floor levels and numerous coins found in stratigraphically significant context, it was possible to date the results with close approximation to precision. Subsequent refinements in the pottery chronology of this period—at first not too well dated—have confirmed the original dates suggested by de Vaux for the Qumran site.[5] The latter had been occupied briefly in pre-Exilic times, but the earliest occupation which could be attributed to the Essenes was dated by coins to a period about 130 B.C. or a little later. There was no clear difference between the pottery of Stratum IA and Stratum IB, and no coins were found in IA. Stratum IB yielded coins of the Seleucid period, three of which can be dated exactly (132-129 B.C.). Other less exactly dated coins of Antiochus VII (138-129 B.C.) and Demetrius II (145-139 B.C.) were also found. Among the bronze coins were five from the reigns of Antiochus III, IV and VII. In the light of the coins it appears that the site was not occupied before the second half of the second century B.C. A single coin from Qumran belongs to the Jewish ruler John Hyrcanus (135-104 B.C.); Judas Aristobulus (104-103 B.C.) is named on another; Alexander Jannaeus (103-76 B.C.) is represented by 143(!) coins. While not all can be dated to a level, there seems little doubt that all belong to Stratum IB.

A date for the foundation of the IB phase after *c.* 100 B.C. seems impossible. Control of the area may still have been effectively in Syrian hands during the first part of John Hyrcanus' rule, as may be indicated by the fact that only one coin of his reign has been identified with certainty. In short, it is possible that the community of Stratum I was founded as early as *c.* 130 B.C., though there is no *certain* evidence of occupation before the last quarter of the century.

The occupation of Stratum IB came to an end with an earthquake and a fire, which can scarcely be separated from one another, as correctly seen by de Vaux. In any case ten coins of the last four Jewish rulers (between 76 and 37 B.C.) before Herod the Great, prove that IB was occupied down to Herod's accession. Fortunately Josephus dates the great earthquake precisely in the year of the naval battle of Actium, 31 B.C., which agrees well with the numismatic evidence. Herod's own attitude toward the Essenes seems to have fluctuated considerably, and since his own great winter palace south of modern Jericho was only about six miles in a straight line from Qumran, he may have decided to move most of the community away even before the earthquake. This would perhaps account for the lack of stratified coins of Herod at Qumran.

The relocation at Qumran by the community of Stratum II has been fixed by de Vaux on strong numismatic evidence (especially a cache of coins dating just before the reoccupation) between 9/8 B.C. and A.D. 1, i.e., at the end of the reign of Herod (37-4 B.C.) or the beginning of the reign of Archelaus (4 B.C.-A.D. 6). Stratum II yielded many coins, extending from Archelaus through the Roman procurators to the third year of the First Revolt (A.D. 68-9). Pottery is abundant in this level; it is identical with that found in Jewish ossuary tombs in the Jerusalem area, as well as with the pottery of the manuscript caves at Qumran. In short, final destruction of the community centre at Qumran came to an end during the Roman invasion of Judaea which laid waste the country around Jerusalem. De Vaux adduces additional convincing arguments for the correctness of his dates, but we lack space even to list them.

3

There seems to be no reason after thirty years to abandon the view put forward (1937) by one of the writers of this essay that the Nash papyrus could be dated, on the basis of material available at the time, to about the second half of the second century B.C., with a possible slight extension downwards. Early in 1948 the same writer was impressed by the remarkable resemblance of the script of the first Isaiah scroll of Qumran to that of the Nash papyrus, and suggested that this scroll be dated at about the same period.[6]

Successive finds in the Qumran area have brought to light a mass of new material for the evolution of the script in question. It soon became possible to arrange successive book-hands and cursive modifications in chronological order, with the latest Qumran scrolls and fragments closely resembling the script of the Uzziah epigraph and a dipinto on a tomb wall, both dating to the last decade or two of Herod's temple (destroyed A.D. 70).

Meanwhile, our external control evidence has increased remarkably, so that both ends of the palaeographical series found in Qumran are bracketed by discoveries at other sites. For want of more precise indications of date, the earliest Qumran fragments had been dated by Frank Cross and Nahman Avigad (before 1963), on the evidence of palaeographical evolution, in the second half of the third century B.C. Since their script is very close to that of the latest Wâdi Dâliyeh documents (dated around 330 B.C.), it is now probable that the oldest Qumran manuscripts date back to the early third century B.C. At the opposite end of the scale we have a fixed *terminus ad quem* at Masada, where numerous inscribed fragments have been found, some quite early, but none later than A.D. 73, when the fortress was stormed by the Romans. Furthermore, the finds at Wadi Murabba'at and Nahal Hever have yielded a quantity of Hebrew and Aramaic material, none of which is later than the end of Bar Kokhba's revolt (A.D. 135), though some goes back to the time of Nero. It is therefore absolutely certain today that the dates given by Cross and Avigad are correct to within very narrow limits.

4

In the light of the preceding survey of the archaeological and palaeographical evidence it is perfectly clear that the latest proposal for a different solution by a scholar of standing—G. R. Driver in his *The Judaean Scrolls: The Problem and a Solution* (Oxford, 1965) —has failed completely. This failure is not caused by any lack of philological learning or of combinatory talent, but to an obvious scepticism with regard to the methodology of archaeologists, numismatists, and palaeographers. Of course, he has had the bad luck to run into head-on collision with one of the most brilliant scholars of our day—Roland de Vaux—and to publish his massive volume just too late to utilize the discoveries at Wâdi Dâliyeh and Masada.

5

No movement which involves the human mind or spirit appears suddenly without prior development; still less do ideas and practices associated with any movement spring from nothing. In fixing the identity of the Qumran sect we must bear in mind the insistence of the sectarians that they alone were the "returned of Israel". From this their concentration on the legitimacy of their priests as "sons of Zadok"[7] is inseparable. To elucidate all this, it is necessary to go back somewhat in time.

The Babylonian exile, often described as the great watershed of Israel's history, may well have seen the first stirrings of classical Jewish sectarianism, and of this we get hints in the memoirs of Ezra and Nehemiah. The latter, judging from his position at court, was almost certainly a eunuch, and this would hardly have been regarded with unmixed approval by orthodox Jews. At the end of his memoirs he laments that he was unable to do more for his people; his main achievement was to restore the city walls of Jerusalem. Ezra, on the other hand, however much he may have been indebted to the work of someone of importance at court such as Nehemiah, self-consciously called himself "the priest, the scribe". It was under his vigorous direction that normative post-exilic Judism began to take shape. What we appear to have here—though it is important not to exaggerate—is the beginning of two attitudes: concern for the physical, national state on the one hand, and concern for a rigid separation of Jews on the other.

The re-establishment of the national state in the late sixth century, followed by the reorganization of temple worship in the late fifth, solved fewer problems than were raised. Babylon had fallen, but the Persian empire did not bring the expected peace to Judah. The new world empire of Macedonia soon broke up into smaller states, which had to be played against one another in order to maintain national existence.

The theme of "sons of Zadok" which appears in the Qumran writings is of considerable importance, even though we are not in a position to trace all its lineage. Throughout the Old Testament there is a thread of concentration on the role of Zadok in the succession of Solomon, and also—indirectly—on the Temple. There is no reason to doubt the tradition that the Zadok who was in David's court and who anointed Solomon, was a descendant of the Shilonite priesthood (I Chron. 6.1-8), tracing his descent (as did Eli) from Ithamar, the younger one of Aaron's two surviving sons. Moreover, once the Temple was in being and was also the repository of the Ark of the Covenant, there would be attached to ministering clergy in the

Temple a prestige which could never have been true of other priests at other shrines in the country. Interest must have quickened in any "legitimizing" ancestry which might secure tenure for those who ministered in the royal capital. In process of time, and in conscious opposition to the northern priesthood after Jeroboam I of Israel, this attitude will inevitably have hardened. Already we have a solid and lasting link between the temple and the "sons of Zadok". The flight of northern priests to the south after 733 B.C. in the face of the Assyrian threat, may well have hardened legitimist attitudes, even while providing additional candidates for inclusion among the sons of Zadok.

The attitude of Ezekiel during the Babylonian exile must be noted here. His future temple is an idealized restoration, and he pictures vividly the "glory" of Yahweh departing—albeit reluctantly—from the Jerusalem temple (Ezek. 10). Perhaps he was a northerner himself: his passionate concern for the ingathering of "all Israel", north and south, a lack of interest in the Solomonic temple which may be discernible in Ezek. 10, a vision which seems more akin to an Assyrian massacre than to a Babylonian deportation (Ezek. 37), all seem to point in that direction. However this may be, his claim that in his ideal restored temple only "sons of Zadok" were to officiate is quite clear. Ezek. 40. 46; 43. 19; 44. 15; 48. 11 clarifies his position. The Greek of the Septuagint reads "sons of *Saddouk*", and this is important for later developments.

In the atmosphere of the reform movement after the exile the question must have been raised as to whether simple physical descent marked a son of Zadok, or whether there were other considerations too. The first short flowering of messianic fervour in the reign of Darius I of Persia found Haggai (Hag. 1. 2) pleading the urgency of the task of restoring the temple, and here a son of Zadok is being urged to go about his proper business. What happened to this attempt we do not know, and it is likely that the Persians cut down this movement as being over-exuberant in its nationalism.

Nehemiah made much use of the sons of Zadok in his work (Neh. 3. 4, 29; 10. 21; 11. 11; 13. 13) and Ezra took care to present his credentials in this respect. Nehemiah's establishment of priestly practice was enough to guarantee its application throughout the Persian empire, as the letter to Elephantine (419 B.C.) testifies. Ezra soon found that Nehemiah's city wall was no guarantee of the integrity of the marriage laws, and there were priests who had contracted marriages with alien women. We may with some confidence assume that one result of the reforms of Ezra was to spread disaffection. There were sons of Zadok dispossessed by reason of alien marriage on the one hand, and on the other zealots dissatisfied with the restoration of such priests after sacrificial restitution. Perhaps here we have the beginnings of that Essene emphasis on the true Israel, later to be allied with second century B.C. pietism.

The crusading zeal of Hellenism left no room for neutralism in the new Jewish state, and attempts to impose religious and political norms by the Seleucids and the Ptolemies produced predictable reactions among Jews. Such attempts appear also to have provided us with the growth of what is now extra-canonical literature. Qumran and Masada have left us texts and fragments of Enoch, Jubilees, the Testaments of the Twelve Patriarchs and Ecclesiasticus. These works belong chiefly to the second century B.C.[8] Enoch may in part be older,[9] while Jubilees (cherished for its calendrical detail) has been dated before *c.* 175 B.C.[10] The Testaments [11] provide us with an important thread in the many-stranded belief of Qumran, for in that work we have the first clear statement of two messiahs, one ecclesiastical ("of Aaron"), and the other civil ("of David"). With the restoration of the monarchy at best an academic issue the climate was ripe for a future idealized messiah, and—on the civil level—a ruler clearly subordinate to the one focal point of loyalty, the priesthood. (*N.B.*, on the necessity of something tangible as a focal point of loyalty, see now Robert Ardrey, *The Territorial Imperative*, New York, 1966, esp. pp. 305ff. on Israel.)

As we come down into the second century (say between 175 and 160 B.C.) the *ḥasîdîm*, "pious ones", appear on the scene, and it was their devotion to the Law which led to the Maccabean revolt against Syrian overlords.[12] We can only imagine the bitterness engendered, after all the high hopes evoked by the success of the revolt, by the realization that the Maccabean (or Hasmonean) rulers were mainly interested in civil independence and civil power. Of itself, such bitterness was unlikely to produce the exclusiveness of the sectarians, and here the influence of Ben Sira may well have been decisive. The author, casting around for some national figure around whom loyalty might coalesce in difficult times, rejected the monarchy, and (surprisingly to us) the prophets too. In part, the cessation of both institutions in Israelite life might account for this, added to the fact that in the Old Testament the term "the righteous one" is applied only to Noah and Abraham (Gen. 6. 9; 7. 1). Ben Sira finds his type of the "Righteous One" in Simon the Just, the high priest who flourished a generation or more before the composition of Ben Sira's work. The priesthood was the only constant element in the national life which had not ceased, and which had not (as had been both monarchy and the prophetic schools) been characterized by rebellion.

Ben Sira's eulogy of Simon (Ecclus. 50), along with the statement that the covenant with Phineas endures, and that his descendants have the priesthood for ever (Ecclus. 45. 24) is all the more pointed when set alongside Ben Sira's disparagement of the monarchy and dismissal of the prophets. In the fragmented state of Judaism at the time, and in the deceptive calm before the Seleucid persecution, only an historical figure of unimpeachable integrity would serve. Simon, whom all our sources (including Josephus) agree in regarding as a good man who ruled wisely, was an identifiable *saddîq*, and not —like Noah or Abraham—belonging to the remote ages. It is also possible that this kind of attention paid to the priesthood may have played a role in the parting of ways between those pietists whose focus of loyalty was the Law, and those who looked to more visible rallying-points.

Of special interest in Ben Sira is the expression which he gives to a determinism which was part of the climate of his times, reflected in Stoicism, astrology, etc. This principle finds expression in both Pharisaism and Essenism. Ben Sira was obviously studied in more circles than one, and he continued to be read long after his time (as evidenced by the discovery of a Hebrew manuscript of the work at Masada, as well as by numerous quotations in rabbinic literature).

The increasing worldliness of the Maccabean high priests after 161 B.C. must have alienated the loyalties of many who claimed to be "sons of Zadok", and in addition to this factor the flight of Jews from Babylonia at the time of the Parthian invasion about 141—140 B.C.[13] merely added to the problems already existing in Judaea. More than one breach in the unity of Judaism was in the making. It is at this point that we may begin to reconstruct Essene history.

It may be safely presumed, on grounds of proximity, that Damascus was a place in which at least one group of Babylonian pietists found refuge after *c.* 140, a place in which to rebuild their lives of devotion. To this period quite certainly belongs the Damascus Document, which does not yet display the concern for celibacy or the rigid dualism which later became so characteristic of Qumran. This was preceded by "twenty years' groping for the way", of which the Document speaks (CD i. 9 f.), before God "raised up for them a Right Guide" (CD i. 11).[14] These two decades may have covered most of the reign of Jonathan (161—143 B.C.), during which the sectarians became increasingly dissatisfied but did not find an effective leader. The Right Guide seems to have organized his sect in Jerusalem, where he was persecuted by Jonathan's brother Simon (143—135 B.C.).[15] The flight to Damascus may have been partly determined by the presence of friends and supporters there, well out of the reach of the authorities in Jerusalem. Not long afterwards the Right Guide died a natural death [16] there. In any case, the settlement at Qumran probably followed the death of Antiochus Sidetes (128 B.C.) and the ensuing conquest of Samaria and invasion of Transjordan by John Hyrcanus.

There may have been a division among the Essenes at this time, one group holding to the old order in which marriage was allowed, and another deriving its less permissive ideas from a source even stricter than the Right Guide. The new community at Qumran, which (judging by the location of female burials on the periphery of the monastic settlement attracted female members from non-celibate groups) began its distinctive sectarian life with the help of extra-canonical (but pre-Essene) literature. The ideas enshrined in the *Manual of Discipline* are obviously the fruit of a period of re-flection and testing, and their partial continuation and development in Christian cenobitic monasticism testifies both to their adaptability and their sanity. The *War Scroll* is not really Essene in character,[17] and is mainly of interest as demonstrating the wide variety of extra-canonical literature studied by the community as bearing on their aspirations and beliefs, and the eschatological element would have appealed to their thinking. Whether the sectarians were engaged in compiling a "canon" of their own is an open question. (Incidentally, the identification of the sect with the Zealots, on the basis of the War Scroll, will not do. As well accuse a Pharisee of being a Hellenist on the score of his use of Greek hermeneutics or Paul of being a Stoic because of his lists of virtues and vices.)

If the style of Qumran commentaries as a method of interpreta-tion (cf. especially the Habakkuk commentary) reflects an older fashion of interpretation (*pesher*) than the Greek-derived rules of hermeneutics (the *middôt*) associated with Hillel the Elder, and perhaps brought by him from Babylonia to Palestine, there is the important element, too, of ritual practice at Qumran. This—ritual lustration, daily, self-administered—may well go back to Babylonian practice.[18] Essene lustrations are attested by Josephus (*B.J.* II. viii. 5, viii. 7; *Antiq.* xviii. 19) and his attestation (since his vindication by archaeology as a generally accurate compiler) is of considerable importance. The climate of Palestine is not such as to favour the practice, and we are driven to posit the origin of this lustration in Babylonian practices.

Another pointer to the origin of the Essenes in the second century B.C. lies in their theology as that is known to us from Qumran. There are so far no Greek loan-words in the Qumran material, but Iranian loan-words are common. Moreover, the prominence of the two spirits governing good, light and truth over against evil, darkness, and falsehood, in the Qumran material can in the end only be explained by reference to the influence of Zoroastrianism at some early point in Essene history. This cannot belong to a time after the second century B.C.

The assertion of an origin in remote antiquity on the part of the Essenes (as recorded by Pliny) demands some kind of explanation, and what we have so far seen provides us with some indications of how they came to hold such a belief. The Babylonian exile saw the crystallization of two view-points, in origin not mutually exclusive, but which led to two divergent attitudes. One concentrated on the Law as the focus of national and religious identity, and here we have the ultimate origin of Pharisaism. The other, lacking this concentration on the Law, tended towards an other-worldly view, stressing apocalyptic revelation. The flowering of apocalyptic certainly encouraged the latter group, as we can see from the Qumran literature.

The prominence of the Zadokite priesthood in the Qumran writings, and the domination of the civil arm by it, is the end of a long process of development, as we have seen. This emphasis on the Zadokite priesthood *may* argue a link with the Sadducees in the past, even though by the time of the Qumran settlement the Essenes had little or nothing otherwise in common with them. Greek *Saddoukaioi* is clearly connected with Ezekiel's insistence (40. 46; 43. 19; 44. 15; 48. 11) on the exclusive rights of the "sons of Zadok" (the LXX has *Saddouk*). He sharply rules out any priests (especially of northern origin) whose lineage might make them suspect in his restoration scheme. Now, whether the Sadducees arrogated the name to themselves because, being "sons of Zadok", they formed the legitimate priesthood, or whether the name was given to them by opponents jealous of their power, we do not know. By New Testament times the name had come to mean adherents of the Hasmonean princes, including priests elevated to the high-priestly dignity by Herod and his successors. More interested in the Temple and the cult than in the Law, the Sadducees nevertheless found themselves on occasion bowing to Pharisaic interpretations of the method of conducting worship. With the Sadducees, contaminated by association with the secular arm (in the Essene view), the Essenes could probably have had few dealings.

With the determinism of the Pharisees, and with their interest in apocalyptic, the Essenes had far more in common. But their rejection of the Temple and with it of the Sadducee priesthood, brought even more sharply into focus the Essene claim to be "sons of Zadok", the true Israel. Here, then, may be the source of the assertion by Pliny and Solinus that the Essene sect was of high antiquity: under the influence of the Right Guide the claim was being made that the sect went back in origin to Solomon's Temple and the original Zadok, just as the Right Guide was endeavouring to restore the *true* temple service.

There is one further observation to be made. Not only was there consuming interest in the legitimacy of the Qumran priesthood as over against the claims of the Jerusalem clergy, but it must also be noted that the Hebrew consonants *ṣdq* can be vocalized to read "the Righteous One", and we are convinced, after considerable study, that the title bestowed on Jesus in Acts 7. 52 has a long and complex history. The fact that such speculations continue to be found at Qumran, and that the Messiah in one document (IV Q Patriarchal Blessings i. 3) is described as "the Messiah, the Righteous One" lends additional weight to our suggestion. There are areas of the New Testament which are best explained as a conscious challenge to Essenism, narrowing still further the concentration on the true Israel, sons of Zadok, or sons of the Righteous One. We plan to examine this subject in some detail on another occasion.

6

So far as is known at present, no literature discovered in the Qumran area makes any mention of the name "Essene",[19] or refers to the sect of the Essenes as such. This fact has, of course, made possible all the speculation which has attended the study of the Dead Sea material, and has led to many identifications of the community at Qumran with various Jewish sectarian bodies. However, we believe that all the literature so far recovered, reinforced by the findings of archaeology and palaeography, makes identification of the community with the Essenes quite certain.

The enhanced reputation of Flavius Josephus as an accurate recorder, thanks to what is now known from Masada, means that his testimony about the Essenes must be taken far more seriously than is sometimes the case. The relevant information is to be found in his *Jewish War* (II. viii. 2—13). Had it not been for the speculation which has surrounded the Qumran material in recent years, it is hard to think that anyone reading Josephus alongside that material could fail to identify the sectarians as Essenes. We have called attention to the evidence of Pliny and Solinus in respect of the Essene rejection of secular pleasure, and Josephus refers to this in emphatic terms, as he does also to their rejection of marriage (2). Both features are well known to us from the Qumran manuscript finds. Prominent in the Dead Sea literature is the tightly-knit hierarchy, with officers for particular duties and oversight, elected from the community. Josephus (6, 10) speaks of this as characteristic of the Essenes. Community of goods and property, known to us as a matter of concern in the Qumran Scrolls, is equally stressed by the same author (3, 4) as a basic concern of the Essenes. Provision for worship in common, with precise directions as to precedence, for common meals, and for common work and the pursuit of crafts— all this is to be found at Qumran. And it is equally to be found in Josephus' account of Essene custom (5, 6). The lustrations which Josephus knew as belonging to Essene custom were also emphasized at Qumran, and there was abundant running water in the ancient oasis for purificatory rites to be accomplished regularly. Qumran had its period of indoctrination and probation, before the aspirant was initiated into the community. Josephus gives us information on the very precise rules which he found among the Essenes, and those rules differ in no particular from those in vogue at Qumran (7). Of the care to preserve books and to study the writings of the ancients there is overwhelming evidence from Qumran: Josephus speaks of all this in the context of the Essenes (6, 7). Brontological fragments at Qumran (from the same source as the later Byzantine Zoroaster) make the interest of the sectarians in divination quite clear. Josephus tells of interest in divination on the part of some Essenes (12). He also tells us that the Essenes were numerous, and that they tended to collect into communities. (The translation of Thackeray, in the *Loeb Classical Library*, here following Whiston, is misleading at this point—II. viii. 4. The Greek does not mean that they "occupied" towns: merely that groups of Essenes would tend to gather into community-settlements.) This grouping into community-settlements we know to have been characteristic of the Dead Sea sectarians (the word in this Damascus Covenant is *maḥanôt*, which means [community] 'settlements" rather than [military] "camps"). Entrusting the initiate with the names of messengers, to which Josephus refers (7), is strikingly illustrated by the occurrence of "resistance names" at Masada and Murabba'at among the Zealots, and this custom may well have been derived from the Essenes. (Cf. the common practice of giving an additional name to members of religious communities at their initiation.)

It is difficult to see, in the face of the evidence of Josephus (not to mention supporting evidence from Pliny and Solinus), what identification of the Qumran community is possible other than an unqualified identification of that community as Essene.

There are other areas of discussion where there is still room for debate, notably in these which concern the background of the New Testament. They may be briefly outlined here. First, there is the title "Son of Man", which figures so prominently in the Gospels. Here it is clear that we must re-translate the Greek by "The Man", in order to do justice to the background of this title. (cf. J. A.

Fitzmyer, S. J., *The "Genesis Apocryphon" of Qumran Cave I*, Rome, 1966, esp. pp. 234f.). What does call for more examination is the ancestry of the term, particularly with regard to the pre-existence of The Man, as this concept is illuminated for us by the saviour-figure of Atrakhasis in the popular cuneiform epic of the last two millennia B.C. (cf. W. F. Albright, *From the Stone Age to Christianity*, N.Y., 1957, pp. 379ff.).[20] Plainly, what Qumran has done for us is to illuminate the New Testament phrase as belonging quite certainly to Messianic ideas in the century before the ministry of Jesus.

The recognition of a system of worship with a minimum of sacrificial observance would appear to be a central feature of the life of the Qumran community. Nevertheless, whether or not the community did have any sacrificial cult at all is still an open question. What does demand more examination is the possible presence of material in the Epistle to the Hebrews which is directed to Christian groups consisting of men who had come under the influence of Essene and Samaritan communities at some time. Since the (as yet largely unpublished)[21] work of the late Abram Spiro on the Samaritans was undertaken, it is of some importance that we do not pass over lightly any references to "Hebrews" in the New Testament. The references to "baptisms", "washings", etc., in the Epistle to the Hebrews tend to argue a reaction to elements in Essene teaching, while the long list of heroes in Hebrews 11 (Solomon is notably absent) may indicate not only a reaction to Essene claims to a long ancestry for their movement, but also may reflect Samaritan antipathy to specifically Jerusalem concerns. The close relation between some Samaritan and Essene groups is now well established.

It is a commonplace of New Testament scholarship that the language of eschatology and apocalyptic in the New Testament writings had its origin in Ezekiel, Daniel, and Enoch. What was lacking was any firm evidence of lines of development in the century before the ministry of Jesus. Qumran has provided us with just those lines of development, but there is now a long and painstaking task before the New Testament scholar. For if Qumran has provided us with much-needed evidence for development of eschatology and apocalyptic, it has also made it abundantly clear that along with the language proper to both there was also a far more complex and varied history of ideas than could have been guessed thirty years ago.

TENTATIVE CHART OF ESSENE CHRONOLOGY

Composition of the *Book of Jubilees*	*c.* 175 B.C.
Composition of most of the *Testaments of the XII Patriarchs*	*c.* 175 B.C.
Early Hasidim	betw. 175 & 160
Composition of *Hôdayôt*	betw. 175 & 160
Jonathan, first high priest of Hasmonean house	161
"Twenty years of groping" (CD)	*c.* 160-140
"Discourses" of Enoch	betw. 175 & 140
Simon, second high priest of Hasmonean house	143
Babylonia overrun by Parthians	141-140
Flight of "Right Guide" and followers to the West	after *c.* 140
Organization of Essene movement	after *c.* 140
Persecution by Wicked Priest	after *c.* 140
Natural death of Right Guide	after *c.* 135
Accession of John Hyrcanus	134
Composition of Damascus Document	after *c.* 134
Flight from Damascus to Qumran	after 128
Probable settlement of Essene community at Qumran	betw. 125 & 100
Composition of Scroll of Discipline	after *c.* 125
Accession of Alexander Jannaeus	104
Probable temporary abandonment of Qumran	betw. *c.* 37-31 and *c.* 9-1 B.C.
Foundation of sect of Zealots by Judas	*c.* A.D. 6-7
Final destruction of Essene monastic settlement at Qumran	A.D. 68-69

2

THE RITES AND CUSTOMS OF
THE QUMRAN SECT

R. K. HARRISON

THE religious community at Qumran consisted of a fellowship of priests and laymen who were pursuing a well-organized communal existence in strict dedication to the will of God. They were bound together by a common desire to aspire to truth and holiness, to study the precepts of the ancient Mosaic Torah, and to foster the ideals and aspirations of the Righteous Teacher, the ostensible founder of the sect. Of all the manuscripts recovered from the Qumran caves, the *Community Rule* (I QS), sometimes known as the *Manual of Discipline*, is by far the most important source of information relating to the nature and organization of the religious brotherhood. This document not merely contained the regulations governing admission to the sect, but furnished in some detail the structure of community life and even prescribed the penalties for various infractions of discipline. An important section of the text recounted the views of the sectaries on the nature of man, and also on the origin and destruction of sin. A devotional composition with which the *Community Rule* concluded threw some light upon the nature of the religious calendar which was observed at Qumran.

By contrast with many other Jewish sects of the day the Qumran brotherhood was rather sternly regimented, and those who desired to be admitted to membership of the wilderness body were required to submit to an exacting preliminary scrutiny. The welfare of the community was supervised by a council of twelve laymen and three priests (I QS. viii. 1), who may have formed the nucleus with which the Righteous Teacher commenced the brotherhood.[1] The formal organization of the community was hierarchical in nature, being categorized into priests, (sometimes known as "Sons of Aaron" or "Sons of Zadok"), Levites, elders, and the ordinary members of the brotherhood.

Periodically a general assembly of the community was held, and in I QS it was described as the "session of the many". Members took their places according to established rules of precedence (I QS. vi. 8-13), with the priests and elders coming first, and strict attention was paid to the standing orders for the conduct of such meetings. Thus the interruption of a speech was deemed as great an offence as speaking out of turn (I QS. vi. 10), and anyone who wished to address the assembly had first to secure permission to do so from the leaders. Certain important questions were decided by the casting of lots, following ancient Israelite tradition, and the whole procedure was supervised by the priests.

One section of the *Community Rule* (I QS. vi. 24—vii. 25) contained the penitential code of the brotherhood, and provided for such breaches of decorum as false statements about property, temperamental behaviour, cursing, indecent exposure, and other forms of unseemly conduct. Punishment generally involved the expulsion of the offender from the "purity of the many" for a stipulated period, and sometimes carried with it a reduction of the guilty person's ration of food. The penalties were graded carefully, and were quite severe in nature.[2] The community was subdivided into camps or settlements, each of which was under the control of an appointed officer. Supervising them all was a chief inspector or *mebaqqer*, whose responsibility it was to see that discipline was maintained throughout the community.

Another prominent official (I QS. vi. 12) examined those who desired to be admitted to membership in the community, posing questions as to their sense of vocation and deciding whether or not to recommend them as suitable candidates. The rules governing the admission of new members were decidedly stringent, and if the candidates satisfied the preliminary enquiries of the interviewing overseer or *paqid*, they then had to appear before the general assembly of the community in order to be formally accepted or rejected. On receiving a favourable decision the candidates had to submit to two further periods of initiation, each lasting for one year and being prosecuted within the confines of the community itself, before enrolment as full members was possible (I QS. vi. 13-23). During the first year of the novitiate they retained their private property, but in the second year their assets were transferred to the custody of the community treasurer (I QS. vi. 20). On being received as recognized members of the Qumran sect, the candidates surrendered their holdings of money and goods to the common fund.

Those candidates who were finally admitted were required to swear a solemn oath to avoid all contact with worldly men, and to return wholeheartedly to the precepts of the Mosaic Torah. This undertaking formed part of an impressive service of full initiation into the sect (cf. I QS. i. 16—ii. 18), conducted by the priests and Levites in the presence of the entire community. The new members were then able to take their proper place in the brotherhood and participate in the sacred meals and purificatory washings which for the first two years had been denied to them in varying degrees.

Because the community was self-supporting, the sectaries worked as agriculturalists, potters, weavers, herdsmen, bee-keepers, and the like, and in this connection it is probable that the oasis of 'Ain Feshkha, some two miles south of Khirbet Qumran, served as the agricultural centre of the brotherhood. Unremitting manual labour thus went hand in hand with sustained piety in the daily routine of the Qumran sectaries, and in this respect they differed but little from some other contemporary pietistic groups in Palestine.

Loyalty to the precepts of the Righteous Teacher was a matter of great importance to the community members, and in consequence they were required to renew their vows at an annual ceremony (I QS. ii. 19-23), at which time those who had honoured their obligations were promoted while delinquent members were penalized (I QS. v. 20-26). Their life was organized in such a manner that specific parts of the day and night were devoted to meditation upon sacred writings and to other spiritual exercises (cf. I QS. x. 1-11. 22). Their dedication to the ancient Law resulted in the formulation of a three-shift system which enabled the Torah to be made a matter of constant study day and night (I QS. vi. 6-7; x. 2) by a specified minimum number of sectaries. The practice of prayer was also of great concern to the covenant community, which observed two principal occasions of daily prayer, namely the evening and the morning (I QS. x. 10). The sabbath also furnished special opportunity for prayer, as did the first day of each month, reckoned according to a solar calendar. If the sectaries followed the pattern of life commonly found amongst similar groups, their normal meals would be eaten in the communal dining hall, and would be of a simple, wholesome character.

It is difficult to say to what extent family life as such obtained at Qumran. The *Community Rule* looked forward to a time when the existence of the entire nation would be properly regulated, so that women and children as well as men could gather together to hear the principles of the covenant law expounded. As far as factual evidence is concerned, the excavation of the cemetery adjacent to the *khirbeh* uncovered a number of skeletons in a poor state of preservation, some of which proved on examination to have been those of females.[3]

The inclusion of women in the community life at Qumran made

for an important difference between the sectaries and the Essenes generally, since the latter almost invariably practised celibacy. There is nothing in the Qumran literature which suggests that full initiation into the sect also involved celibacy or a renunciation of marriage ties, though as Bruce has pointed out,[4] it is difficult to see how those who devoted themselves to the full rigours of community life there could have been able to discharge the normal obligations of marriage and parenthood. But if the community had adherents who lived in the towns and villages of Judea, such individuals would be able to marry and rear families according to the strict Qumranian interpretation of the marriage law. The evidence for this latter, however, is inconclusive, and the general nature and organization of the community seems to militate against it. Although there is no specific directive given on this matter in the Qumran literature, it is probable that candidates who were celibate would be more acceptable generally as community members than those who were married.

Because the organization of the Qumran sect was communal in nature, all properties and possessions were placed in a single category at the disposal of the entire group, and were administered as the need arose by the official appointed for that purpose. While the Qumran neophyte in his first probationary year was forbidden to participate in the communal ceremonies of purification, he was not required to surrender either his money or his property to the *mebaqqer* (I QS. vi. 13-20). If the financial resources of the candidate were recognized at all, they could possibly have been used to defray the expenses of living during the initial year of probation. Once a postulant was admitted, the laws governing the purity of the group would enable him to participate fully in community life and permit his capital resources to be "mingled" with the total assets of the group. If a candidate was deemed unsuitable, his wealth would be returned to him at the end of his probationary period.

The general purpose of the brotherhood was to furnish proper facilities for all who had resolved to turn away from evil and follow the revealed will of God (I QS. v. 1) to implement their desires. In more precise terms the sectaries aimed at attaining that standard of holiness, justice, equity, and mercy which constituted the nature of God as made evident in the ancient Hebrew Scriptures (cf. I QS. v. 3-4). Since God had graciously unfolded the mysteries of propecy to the Righteous Teacher (cf. I QpHab. vii. 3ff.), the sectaries felt confident of their ability to ascertain the divine plan for their lives and for the consummation of the age, an event which they believed would occur within their own generation. Since the Qumran brotherhood had its birth in biblical interpretation, as

Brownlee has put it,[5] the members developed their own explanations of Scripture under the guidance of the Righteous Teacher.

The principal reason for the existence of the group was to prepare for the coming of the Lord through personal submission and diligent study of the Torah, and to this end they worked and worshipped, hoping for the dawn of the Messianic period (I QS. ix. 9-10). The sectaries described themselves as "volunteers for holiness", and as such they submitted to a rigorous discipline which far outstripped the traditions of the Pharisees. In one sense they were endeavouring to make amends for the misdeeds of the latter, feeling as they did that the Pharisees had betrayed their spiritual trust. In consequence the brotherhood looked forward eagerly to a new Jerusalem and a new Temple, where sacrifices acceptable to God would be offered up by a priesthood worthy of this high responsibility.

Their sense of purpose in relationship to their fellow Jews can be illustrated best of all by reference to the most impressive of all their tenets. This was their avowed belief that it was incumbent upon them to make expiation for the wrongdoings of their compatriots (I QS. v. 6) by the purity and dedication of their lives. Because the community thus arrogated to itself an important cathartic function, it felt able to purify those who joined it by absorbing them into its life and discipline. The members believed firmly that their endurance of suffering, their single-minded devotion to the Torah and their submission to severe discipline would be acceptable to God as an atonement for the sins of the nation which had strayed so far from the path of spiritual rectitude.

Such atonement would be effected when the sectaries observed those conditions of repentance and purification which God demanded as prerequisites to forgiveness (cf. I QS. iii. 6; viii. 6; xi. 14). In short, their duty towards contemporary society lay, at its highest level, in fulfilling the role appointed for the obedient, suffering servant of God in Isa. 52. 13—53. 12. With divine help they had determined to make this their avowed objective, and the precepts of the Righteous Teacher were an invaluable guide to this end.

But in addition to propitiation, they were convinced that the task of executing judgment would be their prerogative also. Those who had deliberately perverted justice and spirituality would receive due punishment in the coming day of vengeance (cf. I QS. iv. 12). The sectaries saw no inconsistency between their propitiatory office and the execution of judgment upon the wicked, for in addition to functioning as the divine servant of Isaiah they were also realizing the figure of "one like a son of man" (Dan. 7. 13f., 22), who received authority to judge and exercise universal dominion. They saw what a great many subsequent interpreters have missed, namely that the visionary figure in Daniel was but another aspect of the Isaianic servant, a fact made clear in the teachings of Jesus (cf. Mark 9. 13; 14. 62), and were also aware that such a lofty vocation demanded strict submission and complete righteousness on their part.

The sectaries laid great emphasis upon ritual purification through washing in water, though just how far the ceremonies were actually carried out in the settlement itself is unknown.[6] Excavations at Khirbet Qumran have revealed the lengths to which the community had gone in order to ensure that a proper supply of water would always be available, and it may be that a cistern situated near the southern wall of the main community building served as a baptistry. This particular structure had a number of steps which went down into the water, and seems to have been designed in such a manner as to regulate access to and from the pool itself. On the other hand, the sectaries may have preferred to celebrate their acts of lustration in the "living waters" of the Jordan, or possibly in the oasis area of 'Ain Feshka to the south.[7] At all events, the emphasis at Qumran was placed, not upon the location of the water or the form which the ceremony took, but upon the spiritual implications of the rite itself. In I QS. v. 13-14 it was made clear that true spiritual repentance was the sole factor which determined whether or not a person was cleansed as a result of the lustration. In I QS. iii. 4-9 it was again stressed that water alone would not avail for cleansing in any *ex opere operato* fashion, for this could only be achieved by complete submission of the individual life to the law and will of God. The kind of cleansing which they advocated was that sprinkling with water, that bestowal of an obedient mind, which God promised to his people in Ezek. 36. 25-27. Ritual ablutions at Qumran were emphasized as a consistent element of community life, but despite the spiritual interpretation of the ceremony there is nothing in the literature of the sectaries which would suggest that they required their initiates to undergo a formal baptism of repentance for the forgiveness of sins.

In this sense, therefore, they differed significantly from the practices of both John the Baptist and the primitive Christian Church, and appear to have had considerably more in common with the ritual lustrations of contemporary Judaism. So characteristic of the Qumran sect do such washings seem to have been that the fellowship was commonly described by the title "the purity of the many". It would appear from their writings that they alone of their contemporaries felt able to appreciate the spiritual significance of the baptismal rite, presumably because of the special religious insights which God had given to the Righteous Teacher.

By indulging in such lustrations the sectaries claimed to receive sanctification of the spirit and the power to walk blamelessly in the Torah of God (cf. I QS. iii. 4-9). Because it was the Spirit of God which in actuality cleansed a person from spiritual and moral defilement, the sanctifying of the individual was entertained as a gradual process rather than an immediate act, and one which would be completed by a direct imposition of divine grace at the judgement. Baptism by the Holy Spirit of God was thought by the Qumran sectaries to have been bestowed upon the Messiah in order to pre-vent contamination by evil forces (I QS. iv. 21-22) and also upon his anointed followers (cf. I QS. ix. 11), since the Messiah was to "sprinkle many nations".

There is no hint in the Qumran literature as to precisely how these purificatory rites were to be conducted. As long as an adequate amount of water was available, the ablutions could be carried out in proper conformity with the ideals of the *Community Rule* with-out any need for specific directions as to the mode which was to be employed. There seems little doubt that this same degree of freedom also obtained among other contemporary baptist sects in Palestine, so that an act of ritual cleansing in water would be equally valid whether it was characterized by affusion, immersion, or some other technique. Unless sprinkling was prescribed, the ritual washings of the Old Testament were most probably by total immersion, a method used for the later proselyte baptisms.[8]

Of the varied communal activities of the brotherhood, the meals were given special emphasis as representing the character of the fellowship enjoyed at Qumran. If the sect was actually Essene in nature, an assumption which is by no means certain,[9] the principal meals of the day would be of a simple nature in which all who were eligible and well enough to attend would participate in the com-munal dining room. However, the fellowship of the brotherhood was not completely disrupted if all the members were not present, for the *Community Rule* prescribed that the functions of the sect could be carried out adequately with a quorum of ten members only, one of whom had to be a priest (I QS. vi. 3-4). In gathering together for a meal, whether as a small or large group, the presence of a priest was important since it was his duty to pronounce a benediction before the food was eaten.

Quite apart from the ordinary communal meals, there were special repasts of a more sacramental character. In a fragment from the first Qumran cave which comprised almost two columns of text closely related to, if not an actual part of, the *Community Rule*, the sacred communal meal at Qumran was given a Messianic character by the inclusion in the assembly of the personage of the divinely appointed one, who gave a second benediction to supplement the one pronounced earlier by the presiding priest. In view of the unique destiny which the sect entertained for itself, it may be that the rite had been drawn up as an anticipation of the Messianic banquet which was expected to take place once the new age of grace had dawned. Such a repast would be attended by the priestly and Davidic Messiahs mentioned in the Qumran literature, by the elders and sages of Israel, and by the members of the faithful congregation. This secret meal consisted of bread and wine.

As has been observed earlier, candidates for admission to the community were not allowed to participate in the religious meal immediately, but only after the second year of probation had been completed. This precaution served to illustrate the importance which the Qumran sectaries laid generally upon the concept of the priesthood and its attendant privileges, and it is possible as a concomitant of this attitude that the special communal meal comprised a continuation of the weekly eating of the "bread of the presence" or shewbread (cf. Mark 2. 26).

As such it would constitute a modified form of the ancient Hebrew ritual (Lev. 24. 5-9) in which twelve loaves were replaced each sabbath day before the invisible divine presence on a table, which also held other symbols of a meal such as plates, dishes, and flagons (Exod. 25. 29). That the Pentateuchal traditions concerning priestly perquisites were also taken seriously may perhaps be indicated by the discovery of collections of animal bones at Qumran, buried in association with pottery fragments. The bones came from cattle, sheep, and goats, particularly the latter, and their careful disposal suggests that they had been used in conjunction with special meals. However, the question as to whether the Qumran sectaries actually practised sacrifices or not is difficult to answer. Under ordinary circumstances all sacrificial celebrations would have taken place in Jerusalem. But since the Temple was under the temporary control of an illegitimate high priesthood, according to the views of the brotherhood, it would be impossible for the latter to participate in religious exercises there. It is conceivable, of course, that the men of Qumran erected an altar in the wilderness in the tradition of their ancestors in the time of Moses, on which their own priests offered acceptable sacrifices to God. On the other hand, they may have dispensed with the idea of sacrificial worship altogether, in the conviction that the praises of pious dedicated lips constituted an adequate sacrifice to the Creator. While it is difficult to be certain about this matter, the fact remains that the *Community Rule* contained no instructions with regard to sacrifices. As a result, it may well be that the covenanters of Qumran regarded as their primary concern the offering of their whole personalities to God (I QS. ix. 2-6).

Another marked feature of life at Qumran was its organization in terms of a complex religious calendar. In contrast to the lunar calendar used in Rabbinic circles, the one followed by the sectaries was based on a solar cycle, and consisted of three hundred and sixty four days divided into four sections of thirteen weeks each to correspond with the seasons. A manuscript fragment recovered from the fourth Qumran cave and entitled *The Book of the Priestly Courses* shows that this calendar was identical with the one described in the Book of Jubilees 6. 23ff., and 1 Enoch 72—82. It also furnishes further evidence of the priestly interests of the group, and shows that they had organized a rota of priests similar to that which obtained at the Temple in Jerusalem. At Qumran there were twenty-six divisions, as compared with the twenty-four of 1 Chron. 24. 1—19, each section serving for one week in each half-year of twenty-six weeks, and thus entering upon a week of duty twice annually. While the form of the Qumran calendar had certain contemporary features, the tradition which it preserved was remarkably ancient, and had evident ties with the Temple and the Zadokite priesthood.

The section of the *Community Rule* dealing with conditions for entry into the brotherhood (I QS. i. 16—ii. 18) contained a confession and a series of undertakings given by those being admitted to membership, and also included liturgical directions for the conduct of the ceremony at which these promises were made. This covenant was required to be renewed annually by all members (I QS. ii. 19), an occasion which seems to have constituted one of their principal religious festivals. On the basis of a solar calendar it would be most probably identical with the Feast of Weeks, or Pentecost.[10]

It may well have been given its distinctive covenantal character by the Qumran fellowship from the nature of the Old Testament passages read on that occasion, particularly if the Talmudic tradition (*Meg.* 31a) is correct in maintaining that Exod. 19 was read in the lectionary on the Feast of Weeks. This covenantal emphasis was entirely in accordance with the desire of the sectaries to return to the traditions of Moses, and the ritual associated with the annual renewal of vows is quite similar in character to that of Deut. 27—30. While their concept of a new covenant was one which had to be entertained with conviction (I QS. ii. 11-18) and engraved for ever upon the mind (I QS. x. 6, 8), it was still the old covenant in renewed form, bound to the Law as a body of precepts to be observed with due care.

The first day of each month as determined by the solar calendar was set aside at Qumran as a time for prayer (I QS. x. 5). This day seems to have been given equal importance with the sabbath for purposes of worship and private devotion. For the sectaries, the beginning of each month was a token that the eternal mercies of God were being renewed, and indicated that the divine plan for the end of the age was being prosecuted steadily, even though there might be little tangible evidence of that fact.

These occasions were required to be observed as memorials and holy days, an emphasis which was thoroughly consistent with the nature of a covenant community (cf. Exod. 20. 8). Prayer was also enjoyed on what might be called the "intercalary days" (I QS. x. 3-5), at which the seasons succeeded one another (cf. Book of Jubilees 6. 23-28). Apparently two of the days were equinoxes and two were solstices. According to the calendar of worship contained in I QS. x. 1-8, prayer and praise were to be offered to God on the following occasions. (a) every day (x. 1-3a); (b) the intercalary days of the solar year (x. 3b-5a); (c) the first day of each month and the sabbath days (x. 5b-6a); (d) the intercalary days of the solar year, being described differently from the language used in x. 3b-5a; (e) festival years at the end of seven-year periods, and jubilee years.

At Qumran the "feasts of years" (I QS. x. 8a) embraced every seventh and fiftieth year, the concept of the former being based upon the idea of a seventh year sabbath in Lev. 25. 1ff. The jubilee system was of ancient origin, and was related to the processes of history in the same sense that the calendar was concerned with the recording of more immediate temporal sequences. This conception of history involved a series of fifty-year epochs in which the final year of each cycle was marked by celebrations including the remission of debts, the return of property to its original owners, and the release of enslaved Israelites.

Laudable as this concept was, there is unfortunately very little evidence that it was ever observed to any extent by the Israelites. In the Book of Jubilees the last year of the jubilee cycle formed the first year of the following epoch, so that actually the jubilee was computed in terms of seven times seven years. This method brought it into much closer affinity with the calendar, since the forty-nine day period from Passover to Pentecost was also arrived at by counting seven times seven.

The "feasts of years" were very important elements in the Qumranite conception of history. On the basis of the reckoning in the Book of Jubilees, the fiftieth cycle computed from Anno Mundi 2402, saw the deliverance of the Israelites from Egypt and the giving of the Sinai covenant. With this important event commenced the era of the Law, and as far as the author of the Book of Jubilees was concerned this epoch could only terminate with the appearance of God upon earth and the inauguration of a new age of grace. This latter concept was an essential part of the beliefs of the Qumran sectaries, who were convinced that they were living at the time when the era of the Law would come to an end. This was one of the principal reasons why they withdrew into the desert in order to build a highway for their God (I QS. viii. 12-18). It would seem clear, then, that in their calendar of worship the brotherhood sought to redress that imbalance of neglect which had evidently overtaken the jubilee cycles in Israel, since for them the end of the current period would usher in the liberation of the true, spiritual Israel and witness the restoration of divine worship by a purified nation.

In all their rules and customs the Qumran sectaries sought to exemplify the ideals of legalistic piety, rigid discipline, obedience to the divine will, and submission to the ethos of the ancient Mosaic Law. Their expectation of a Messiah was more consistent with the Old Testament picture in a great many respects than was that of contemporary Judaism. However, while it has been maintained with some justification that the early Christian heretical sects in Palestine took their rise in part from the dispersed members of the sect, the actual extent to which the Qumran brotherhood recognized the historical Christ is uncertain.

3

THE TEACHER OF RIGHTEOUSNESS
AND THE MESSIAH(S)

RAYMOND E. BROWN

THIS chapter treats two different aspects of Qumran thought. The Qumran references to the Teacher of Righteousness evoke memories of the past, for the man so entitled was the founding father of the community, its hero and ideal. The Qumran references to the Messiah(s) express hope for the future, for the day when God brings forward the Messiah(s) will be the day for him to accomplish his plan for the true Israel.

THE TEACHER OF RIGHTEOUSNESS

We must introduce this figure by describing the historical situation that was the background of his life.[1] It was during the reign of the Syrian king Antiochus Epiphanes (175—163 B.C.) that there emerged the religious reform movement that would ultimately engender the Qumran sect.[2] The forefathers of Qumran were probably the group called Hasidim or "pious ones" who aligned themselves with Mattathias, the father of Judas Maccabeus, in the revolt of 167 against the Syrian tyrant (1 Macc. 2. 42). Their motivation was primarily religious; they were incensed at the blasphemies committed by the Hellenized Jews favorable to Antiochus and, in particular, at the removal from office of Jason, the legitimate high priest of the line of Zadok, in favor of Menelaus, a non-Zadokite, in 172 (2 Macc. 4. 23–26). The support that the Hasidim gave to the Maccabean revolt was not undivided; for the Maccabees combined the political with the religious until finally their dynastic ambitions sullied the purity of the cause for which they fought. We see an indication of the friction between the two groups in 1 Macc. 7. 9–16. When the Syrians appointed the treacherous Alcimus as high priest, the Hasidim accepted him because he was "a priest from the line of

37

3

Aaron", while Judas Maccabeus took the shrewder political course
of rejecting him.

The events of the year 152 probably caused the decisive break
between the Hasidim and the Maccabees. In that year Jonathan, the
brother and successor of Judas, accepted appointment as the high
priest (1 Macc. 10. 18-21). This action by one who was not from
the line of Zadok must have constituted an unforgivable sin in the
eyes of those Hasidim who had joined the revolt in the first place
in defence of the Zadokite priesthood. And so at least part of the
Hasidim separated themselves from the Maccabean movement and
banded together under the leadership of an unnamed Zadokite priest,
perhaps the heir in the direct high priestly line. It is he whom the
Qumran documents call the Teacher of Righteousness.[3] The moment
of his appearance on the scene is described in CD i. 9-11 : after
"twenty years in which they were like blind men groping their
way" (i.e., the years of support for the Maccabees), God "raised up
for them a Teacher of Righteousness to guide them in the way of
his heart".

The separation was not accomplished without bitterness; for the
Teacher was opposed by the "Wicked Priest" who had been faithful
at the beginning of his career but who betrayed the commandments
when he became ruler of Israel (1 QpHab. viii–x)—a description of
Jonathan who had led the revolt for eight years before he assumed
the high priesthood. It was to find shelter from the Priest's hatred
that the Teacher soon led his followers to the wilderness of Qumran.
(Archaeology points to a beginning of settlement at Qumran *c.* 140
B.C.) But there was a theological motive also : here the Teacher's
community could relive the desert experience and purification that
Israel had know a millennium before when it had fled from the
Pharaoh. Henceforth whoever would live among these pious men
would have to observe the precept to "separate from the dwelling
places of the ungodly and go into the wilderness to prepare the way
of God, as it is written : 'Prepare in the wilderness the way of the
Lord; make straight in the desert a path for our God' " (1 QS. viii.
13-14). The migration to Qumran *may* be described symbolically
in CD vi. 4—9 which speaks of "the converts of Israel who went out
of the land of Judah to sojourn in the land of Damascus". According
to CD the movement was prompted by the "Interpreter of the Law",
seemingly the Teacher (see also CD vii. 19 discussed below).

Yet even in his desert retreat the Teacher faced trials. On the
sacred Day of the Atonement (Yom Kippur)[4] the Wicked Priest
pursued the Teacher to his place of exile (1 QpHab. xi. 4-8). Finally,
however, God delivered the Teacher and punished the Wicked
Priest by handing him over to the Gentiles for judgement—if this is

the correct interpretation of I QpHab. ix. 9-12 and IV QpPs. 37 I. 18-20, it fits the career of Jonathan who was arrested in 143 B.C. by the Syrian general Trypho and died in prison (1 Macc. 12. 48; 13. 23). But Simon, the brother and successor of Jonathan, widened the split between the Maccabean dynasty and the followers of the Teacher; for in 140 B.C. Simon accepted the high priesthood for himself and his children *forever* (1 Macc. 14. 41-48), thus irrevocably abrogating the Zadokite claims. The text of the Psalms of Joshua, preserved in IV Q Test. xxi–xxix, condemns Jonathan and Simon together: "Behold an accursed man, a man of Belial, has risen to become a snare to the people and a cause of destruction to all his neighbours. And [his brother] arose [and ruled], both being instruments of violence." [5] Seemingly the Teacher outlived both his Maccabean enemies and died during the reign of Simon's son John Hyrcanus (135—104 B.C.). Our only evidence for this is that CD, probably written *c.* 100 B.C., places an interim of about forty years between the Teacher's death (past) and the (apparently future) destruction of the men of war who deserted to the Liar—but is the number forty to be taken literally?

The above reconstruction of the career of the Teacher, partially hypothetical, is based on the few facts that we know about him. (It is interesting that any one Gospel gives us more information about Jesus, including his name, than all the more abundant Qumran literature gives us about the Teacher!) But his real character stands forth more clearly in the impact he left on those who followed him. He was evidently a man of deep personal piety. Many scholars regard him as the author in whole or in part of the Qumran hymnal (QH).[6] If this is true, the hymns show him to have been profoundly conscious of his mission, aware of his weakness and dependence on God, but filled with trust in God's destiny for him. Speaking to God, he describes himself as one "into whose mouth You have put doctrine and into whose heart You have put wisdom that he might open a fount of knowledge to all intelligent men" (ii. 17-18). "Through me You have given light to the face of many and have shown Your infinite power, for You have instructed me in Your marvellous mysteries" (iv. 27-28). "I thank You, O Lord, for You have upheld me by Your strength and have poured forth Your holy spirit upon me" (vii. 6-7). "You have made me a father to the pious" (vii. 20).

If he was a Righteous Teacher himself, he also taught others righteousness. Whether or not he composed the Qumran Rule of Life (QS), as some maintain, the Teacher set the basic pattern of the community's distinctive behaviour and thought. When the Qumran writings insist that the sectarians must observe the Law, they mean the Law as it was interpreted by the Teacher, who was also known as the Interpreter of the Law.[7] In I QpHab. viii. 2-3 the community is described as those "whom God will deliver from the house of judgement because of their suffering and *because of their faith in the Teacher of Righteousness*".[8] Also the Teacher knew God's plan for the salvation of men, for God had revealed to him how the words of the prophets were being fulfilled in and through the Qumran community (I QpHab. vii. 3-5).

The Teacher's piety amidst persecution and his influence on his community have been compared to the piety and influence of Jesus. And certainly the unnamed Teacher would seem to have been one of the noblest of the many figures in Israel whom Christians designate as forerunners of Jesus. But it is truly irresponsible to the evidence to present the Teacher as a carbon copy of Jesus or, worse, to claim that Jesus was only a copy of the Teacher. The theology of the Teacher differed from that of Jesus in its most basic emphases. The Teacher was vitally interested in the purity of the priestly line, in following a sacred solar calendar, and in the strictest observance of the Law, none of which seems to have concerned Jesus at all. If Jesus' mission was to proclaim the rule of God even to sinners, the Teacher drew men away from ordinary life to join an isolated community of saints. Jesus' followers claimed that he had saved men by his death and resurrection. There is no evidence that the Teacher suffered a violent death at the hands of his enemies, much less that he was crucified.[9] The suggestion that the Teacher was raised from the dead is pure fantasy.

What evaluation did the Teacher put on his own career? We have seen that he regarded himself as one to whom God's mysterious plan of salvation had been revealed, but we are not certain that he thought of himself as an eschatological figure. He speaks of his suffering, but we are not certain that he thought of himself as the Suffering Servant. Whereas the followers of Jesus exalted their master as the Messiah and Son of God, no Qumran document ever calls the Teacher a Messiah; indeed CD xix. 35—xx. 1 distinguishes between the death of the Teacher and the still future coming of the Messiah(s). It is not impossible that the Teacher's followers hoped at first that God would deliver them during the Teacher's lifetime, but after he died they certainly thought of the eschatological intervention as still to come. By way of contrast, even after Jesus' death, his followers continued to believe that the eschatological era had really come in his ministry.

THE MESSIAH(S)

We turn now to a topic that is more difficult because of the vagueness of what is designated by scholars as messianic. It is quite clear that in late Judaism there were varied expectations about the figure(s) whom God would send to inaugurate or implement his supreme intervention on behalf of Israel. In the New Testament and the Jewish pseudepigrapha the following are mentioned : the Davidic Messiah, the Prophet (like Moses), a prophet (e.g., Jeremiah), Moses, Elijah, the Son of Man, the Elect One (= the Servant?), and Michael. Of course, there is also a strain of Jewish literature that hopes for God's direct intervention without mentioning any intermediary, human or angelic. Sometimes all these expectations have been spoken of as messianic, so that "messianic" becomes almost a synonym for eschatological. Here we shall confine "messianic" to that form of eschatological expectations which speaks explicitly of the Messiah(s), i.e., of one or more specific *anointed* salvific figures in the last days.[10] This understanding of messianism seems to conform to Qumran's own outlook; for instance, I QS. ix. 11 distinguishes the eschatological prophet from the Messiahs of Aaron and Israel; Michael, who leads the forces of good in victory over Satan in the final war, is certainly an eschatological figure but is never called a Messiah. Our method will be to treat the relatively clear messianic references of the Qumran literature [11] in chronological order, thus allowing for the possibility of change or development in Qumran expectations. We shall find the evidence sparse, but the references to a Messiah in the Jewish pseudepigrapha contemporary with the Qumran literature are also scarce. We caution also that the unpublished Cave 4 material will eventually fill out and modify the outline we give below.

In the earliest Qumran literature (140—110 B.C.) there is no reference to a Messiah. The literature of this period is not abundant; but its silence on Messianism is significant because Cave 4 copies of QS are involved, and the later copy of this work from Cave 1 does refer to the Messiah(s). This period saw the work and career of the Teacher of Righteousness; and perhaps it was only as he grew old or even after his death that there was intense reflection on the future of God's plan and on how the final intervention would be brought about.

In any case it is in the writings of the period 110—70 B.C., presumably just after the Teacher's death, that we find the first clear expression of messianic expectation. The most important and probably the earliest text that we have on the subject is I QS. ix. 11, dating from *c.* 100 B.C. The author insists on the necessity of keeping the community's laws "until the coming of a [the] prophet and the Messiahs of Aaron and [of] Israel".[12] The plural has suggested to most scholars that two anointed figures were expected: one a priest of the Zadokite line representing Aaron, and the other a layman of the royal Davidic line representing Israel. That there were at Qumran expectations of two important eschatological figures, one priestly and one Davidic, has been confirmed by other writings contemporary with I QS. In the "Rule for All the Congregation of Israel in the Last Days" (I QSa) a banquet is described where the two who preside are entitled the Priest and the Messiah of Israel. The group of blessings called I QSb, apparently intended for the last days, has a blessing that seems to fit the Priest and a blessing for "the Prince of the Congregation." The latter is probably the Davidic Messiah, as we may determine from a comparison of the context with other Qumran works[13] and also from Ezekiel's use of "prince" for the Davidic ruler.

The works we have discussed thus far have a unity, at least in the sense that they were all written on one scroll. Do other Qumran documents of this period share the expectation of the two Messiahs, or was there diversity within the community's thought? The evidence of CD (from *c.* 100 B.C.?)[14] is important here, for it seems to have been written for a form of sectarian life slightly different from that envisaged in I QS. We begin with the specific messianic references in CD. It mentions "a Messiah of Aaron and Israel" (xii. 23—xiii. 1; xiv. 19; xix. 10-11) and "a Messiah from Aaron and from Israel" (xx. 1). These expressions could *possibly* be interpreted to refer to two Messiahs: a Messiah of or from Aaron and (a Messiah) of or from Israel; but this is not the obvious grammatical import of the expressions. (One is tempted to use the clear expression for two Messiahs in I QS as a guide here, but that would be to confuse the question that we are raising about the unanimity of thought.) The more obvious references of the expressions in CD would be to one Messiah representing both Aaron and Israel. The situation in CD could be clarified in favour of the former of the above interpretations if we found elsewhere in the document the expectation of two salvific figures, one priestly and one Davidic. One passage that suggests itself is CD vii. 18-20 which supplies a pesher interpretation of Num. 24. 17. We are told that the *Star* that shall step forth out of Jacob is "the Interpreter of the Law who came [shall come?] to Damascus," while the *Sceptre* is "the Prince of the whole Congregation." Clearly there are two figures here. The first is priestly, for interpreting the Law is a priestly function (see *Test. Levi* 18. 3); the second has a ruling function and indeed elsewhere his title seems to refer to the Davidic Messiah. But we cannot be sure that in this passage CD is speaking about the future. The Interpreter of the Law who came(?) to Damascus may be a reference to the Teacher who brought the community to Qumran. Thus, unfortunately, the messianism of CD is not clear; it can be interpreted to harmonize with the messianism of I QS, but we are not certain.

Moving on to a later period of Qumran writing, we come to the War Scroll (QM, probably from 50 B.C.-A.D. 25). This eschatological work gives prominence to the Chief Priest who is put at the head of the Levites and the tribes and even seems to guide the course of the final battle. There is no reference by name to the Messiah of Israel, but I QM. v. 1 mentions the Prince of the whole Congregation. Perhaps he is the combat leader since the priests do not fight. Two figures appear in the pesher on Psalms called IV Q Flor. (A.D. 1-50). It mentions: "The Branch of David who will arise with the Interpreter of the Law . . . at the end of days." The first is the Davidic Messiah; the second exercises a priestly function. In IV QpIs[a] ii. 21-28 there is also a reference to "the Branch of David who shall arise at the end of days"; priests will teach him how to render judgement. Thus, although there is no specific mention of the Messiahs of Aaron and Israel, these late works do seem to have kept alive the twofold messianic expectations.

When we look at this Qumran expectation in the broad context of late Judaism, it is not a difficult phenomenon to explain. The expectation of a future Davidic Messiah was a post-exilic development resulting from the idealization of the anointed king during the monarchy. When the Davidic line no longer ruled, the anticipation that the next king would be the ideal king (e.g., Isa. 7—9) seems to have shifted to the anticipation of a supreme Davidic king who would deliver Israel in or before the last day. But precisely in this post-exilic period, in the absence of a monarch, the anointed high priesthood achieved a political status it had never held before. In Zech. 4. 14 the high priest Joshua and the Davidic prince Zerubbabel are *ex aequo* "the two anointed ones who stand by the Lord". In the canticle appearing in the Hebrew of Sirach after 51. 12 (perhaps a Qumran creation) the house of David and the sons of Zadok are praised one after the other.

The sectarians of Qumran adopted and adapted the traditional belief that God would ultimately raise up a warrior from David's line to deliver Israel, but in their mind the true Israel was the Qumran community which alone was faithful to God's commands. Their expectations were also influenced by the fact that the Teacher, a Zadokite priest, had formed the community. Would God not send another anointed priest in the last days to bless the community and give it a final enlightenment? And so along with the anointed Davidic king they came to expect an anointed high priest who would guide the king. We find a similar expectation in the *Testaments of the Twelve Patriarchs*, a composite work whose origins were contemporaneous in part with the Qumran literature.[15] The thesis of two Messiahs survived into medieval Judaism among the Karaites, a sectarian movement influence by Qumran thought.[16]

Obviously the addition of a Messiah of Aaron gives to Qumran messianism another dimension, different from the more secular hopes centred around the Davidic Messiah. Some of the prophetic dreams of spiritual blessings, especially in terms of instruction, are related to the figure of the Priest. Yet, lest we get too romantic, the Chief Priest also has a military role in the final war. Moreover, neither of the Messiahs emerges as more than a shadowy idealization. It is almost impossible to compare realistically Qumran messianism with Christian messianism, focused completely on Jesus. Some have sought a connection in the idea that the Teacher of Righteousness figures in Qumran messianic expectations, perhaps as the anointed Priest. CD vi. 11 speaks of the coming of him "who shall teach righteousness at the end of days"; and we have seen a reference to the eschatological Interpreter of the Law, a title applicable to the Teacher. However, such details do not require us to believe that the sectarians expected the Teacher to return in the last days; they are explicable with less demand on the imagination if the sectarians had shaped their ideal of the Messiah of Aaron on what they most admired in the Teacher—a Messiah like the Teacher, rather than the Teacher come back to life.

Others have seen similarities between Qumran messianism and the picture of Jesus in the Epistle to the Hebrews; they suggest that the presentation of Jesus, the Davidic Messiah, as a priest represents a fusion of the Qumran ideal of two Messiahs. Without ruling out possible relationship between aspects of Qumran theology and the theology of Hebrews, we would simply point out that in Hebrews Jesus is most definitely not a Messiah of *Aaron*. The whole point is that his priesthood is not Levitic. Moreover his priesthood is related to his sacrificial death, and the idea of sacrificial death (or even of suffering) never appears in Qumran messianism. As far as we can judge from the literature already published, in the question of messianism, *taken alone and strictly understood*, Qumran is not noticeably closer to Christianity than are the other branches of late Judaism

4

ESCHATOLOGY IN THE
DEAD SEA SCROLLS

JOHN PRYKE

Eschatology,[1] or the doctrine of the last or final events of the end of the world, was developed in the hopes and disappointments of the Jewish nation's plight in the Babylonian exile. The defeat and transportation of the leaders of the chosen race was a blow to their faith in the prophetic teaching that Yahweh controlled historical events. While the Law for many continued to suffice as the medium of God's revelation, the apocalyptical writers gave expression to the desire for absolute justice and the coming of God's Kingdom in the inspired fantasies of their literature, and at the same time the struggle for freedom and for the restoration of national sovereignty gave impetus to the Maccabean revolt, and sustained the continuous uprisings of the Zealots during the Christian era.

In the full-blooded eschatology, God in his Heaven is temporarily divorced from his world on earth. The divinity is regarded as so removed from the affairs of men that his sovereignty of the world appears to have been temporarily abandoned to the forces of evil, until the "last days". Meanwhile Satan controls the destiny of men. Angels and demons struggle for ascendancy in the heaven above while the pious have to endure the impious, and Zealot fights against Roman oppression on the earth below. Even the physical universe becomes identified with the wickedness of the human race—hence the necessity for its destruction and recreation. The contemporary age was regarded as an evil time, during which lawlessness and impiety would increase, until the intervention of God shortened it for the sake of his elect. The exact time of his intervention was unknown, but it was believed that he would come suddenly and without warning, each age interpreting for itself the signs of his coming.

Yahweh's return to judge the wicked and to save the pious living and dead by a resurrected life in a new dimension on a recreated Universe is an indispensable article of belief to the apocalyptical school of transcendental eschatology. A series of diagrams will illustrate the differences between the various schools, although over-simplification must not imply that every pattern fits into any of the three suggested types. The thorough-going eschatology may be illustrated by diagram A, and by a quotation from Mowinckel. In the diagrams the straight line, the present evil age, represents normal space-time; the double line represents the second age, eternity. The symbols ● and **X** are special points in time when God intervenes; ● differentiates "historical" eschatology from **X**, "trans-cendental" eschatology.

"Eschatology" writes Mowinckel, "is a doctrine or a complex of ideas about 'the last things', which is more or less organically coherent and developed. Every eschatology includes in some form or other a dualistic conception of the course of history, and implies that the present state of things and the present world order will suddenly come to an end and be superseded by another of an essentially different kind . . . Eschatology also includes the thought that this drama has a universal cosmic character. The universe itself, heaven and earth is thrown into the melting pot. The transforma-tion is definitely catastrophic in character, and is brought about by supernatural, divine, or demonic powers."[2]

Side by side with transcendental eschatology, the various historical eschatologies continued to exist, inspiring the Maccabean move-ment and the Zealot uprisings. In the history of Judaism reformations of the religious life were often closely linked with demands for political independence. God might seem to have abandoned his people to the heathen oppressor, but the apocalyptic visionary sometimes also hoped for a military saviour or king to assist the prophetic or priestly leaders of the reform. His main function was to prosecute the Messianic War, the outcome of which would be a long period of peace and prosperity for the Jewish victors. Such was the limited perspective of historical eschatology, but to the extreme apocalyptical school they were only interim expedients, and sometimes regarded as unnecessary and omitted in their schema. The Messiah they replaced by a completely other-worldly figure, the "Son of Man", who is an angelic or heavenly person, judging the whole world. He is concerned with the life beyond, even if it is to be lived on this earth, *transformed* and experienced in another dimension. Diagram C shows how the thoroughgoing and historical eschatologies are sometimes combined (see p. 47). "According to the Ezra Apocalypse, it is only when the Kingdom of the Messiah is at an end, and the world has returned to

Diagram A: Transcendental Eschatology

Present — Evil Age — X — Last — Things — Wars, destruction of Universe / Resurrection of dead / 'Son of Man' as Judge — Future — Blessed Age (New Heaven and New Earth)

Diagram B: Historical Eschatology

Present — Evil Age — Messianic War (40 years) — Messianic Interregnum (40 or 1000 years peace and prosperity)

Diagram C: Transcendental and Historical Eschatology Combined

Present — Evil Age — Messianic War — Messianic Interregnum — X — Last — Things — Future — Blessed Age

chaos, that the resurrection comes. Then the Most High reveals himself on the throne of judgement, and then comes the end (2 Esdras 7. 33). This is the usual conception in apocalyptic."[3]

In the Jewish apocalyptic literature of the last two centuries before Christ, and in the first century of the Christian era, there may be found a galaxy of references to the "last things". First, and foremost, is the concept of the two ages, the present evil and rebellious age, and the age to come, or the Blessed Age. Between the present and the near, or future, age many possible exigencies are imagined and elaborated. The power and influence of Satan would grow stronger; the suffering of the elect would increase until God sent his anointed one, or ones, to free his people—then the victors could enjoy a thousand years of peace. This is only eschatological in a broad sense, and precise terminology would not allow the use of the word in our third category, which may be illustrated thus (see Diagram B, "Historical Echatology", p. 47).

The assumption that the Qumran sect's eschatology comes under Diagram A or C is by no means as certain as some have assumed. The complete omission of the "Son of Man" in the writings is the first point to be noted, and secondly the obscurity of the texts on the question of the resurrection of the body and the Universal Judgement. The real point of argument in the question of the eschatological beliefs of the sect is to decide how far the sect went beyond category B, if at all. If its aspirations were limited to the Messianic War and interregnum, then the term "eschatological" if applied to its teachings is misleading and inaccurate.[4] The literature of the Pseudepigrapha and the New Testament contains ideas and expressions which are firmly placed in categories A and C. Although certain of the sectarian writings and texts are to be understood also in terms of a real eschatology, the main stream of the literature is in category B, that of historical eschatology. An added difficulty is that the texts on the future life are problematical and by no means encourage dogmatism or speculation.

The Qumran community believed that God had providentially designed history in cycles of time, consisting of two ages: the present age, the "epoch of wickedness", when evil would flourish, and the age to come, which is the period after the Messianic victory, lasting for a thousand years. Psalm 37, iii, 1-2 pesher commentary runs: ". . . the penitents of the desert who shall live for a thousand generations in Israel, and to them all the inheritance of Adam shall belong, and to their seed for ever." The sect thought that its world was approaching the end of one era, and on the verge of a new and better time for them. In the Zadokite Documents, the manual of the open married order of farmers, living in camps, are found references to the present age as the "epoch of wickedness" (CD vi. 10, 14; xii. 23; xiv. 19; xv. 7, 10), the "epoch of Israel's Sin" (xx. 23), the "epoch of the desolation of the land" (v. 20), the "epoch of the punishment of the forefathers" (vii. 21a). From the opening of the "Admonition", the first part of the Zadokite Documents, in an esoteric reference, the movement is dated "390 years after(?) he had given them into the hand of Nebuchadnezzar, in the 'epoch of anger' " (i. 5).

In the manual of the closed celibate order, the Rule of the Community, instructions are given to the priests and levites to give the Blessings and a recitation of all the past favours shewn by God to the community during the "dominion of Belial" (I QS. ii. 19). All those entering the community (at this yearly convenantal ceremony) shall answer and say after them, "Amen! Amen!" (ii. 18) to the blessings and the curses. Members of the community were assigned their rightful place at this meeting, which was to take place annually for as long as the first age, "the dominion of Satan", lasted (ii, 19-25a).

The establishment of the community at the desolate site of Qumran is regarded as the fulfilment of the prophecy of the unknown prophet of the Exile, Second Isaiah.

"And when these become members of the Community in Israel, according to all these plans, they shall cut themselves off from the place of the ungodly men, and shall go into the desert to prepare the way of the Lord; as it is written, Prepare in the wilderness the way of . . . . [= Yahweh, the sacred name, too sacred to be written down] make straight in the desert, a highway for our God" (I QS. viii. 13-14). The "highway" is interpreted by the sect as the study of the Law in perfection which will be an offering (I QS. v. 6; viii. 15) acceptable to the Lord, atoning for the imperfections elsewhere in Judaism. In the same spirit as John the Baptist, in Mark 1. 2-3, who also cited this text, the sect's way of life in retreating from the world, and living in miniature the exact rule of purity is regarded as an appropriate penance for the coming of the Lord who will judge the wicked and justify his elect, the Qumran community.

The Rule contains a discourse on the "Two Spirits in Man", which mankind has been assigned until the time of God's visitation (iii. 13—iv. 14) ". . . so all their sins and their iniquities and their guilt and the transgressions of their deeds are under his dominion (according to God's mysteries), until his end-time; while all their afflictions and their seasons of distress are under the dominion of his hostility".[5] The Devil (the angel of darkness) dominates the sons of darkness (the orthodox Jews and the Gentiles), and sometimes seduces the sons of light (the community). Such dualistic language reflects the community's tension in its struggle against those who did not follow its strict way of living, but reflects primarily its belief that Satan would increase in hostility until the time of divine intervention when the community would produce two leaders to prosecute the victorious Messianic War, the outcome of which is described in glowing terms: "the making of the New" (I QS. iv. 25); ". . . everlasting rejoicing in the victorious life of eternity, and a crown of glory, together with raiment of majesty in eternal light" (iv. 7, 8). The "victorious life of eternity" is a poetic image for the Messianic interregnum; the "crown of glory" is the warrior's reward after the heat of battle. Some expressions in the texts such as "eternal life with the glory of Adam" (CD iii. 20) recall the apocalyptical writers' dream of recapturing man's sinless state of perfection which he was believed to have enjoyed before his fall from grace—probably an argument here in favour of a real eschatology.

Between the two ages, the community would have to undergo the turbulence and upheavals resulting from a dying civilization and the birth of a new one. The "woman in travail" in the 3rd Hymn has been interpreted as the mother of the Messiah giving birth to the saviour; the agonies she suffers in the child-bearing are similar to those of the community which will bring forth from its members the Messianic leaders capable of winning the war of deliverance. Possibly the quotation from a Messianic passage in Isaiah would favour the Messianic interpretation:[6]

> . . . They made [me] to be
> like a ship on the deeps of the [sea],
> and like a city fortress
> in face of the [invader],
> I was like a woman in travail
> with her first-born child,
> upon whom pangs have come,
> and violent pains
> with waves of anguish from her child-bearing furnace.
> For the young have approached the waves of Death,
> and she who bears the man suffers in pains.
> For in the midst of the waves of Death,
> she shall give birth to a man child,
> and amidst the birth-pains of Sheol,
> there shall spring forth from this oven
> a "Wonderful Thing, Counsellor";
> and the Man-child shall be delivered from the waves.
>
> At his conception
> all wombs shall be excited,

and at the time of their giving birth
they shall be in appalling agony;
those who are pregnant
shall be grievously distressed.
And when he is born
every pang shall come upon the child-bearing furnace.

(iii. 6-12)

The Qumran Psalmist, who may have been the Teacher of Righteousness, likens the community's sufferings to the birth-pangs of the mother of the Saviour Deliverer, and asserts that out of the agonies of the sectarians' persecutions would the Messianic leader arise. But in the opening stanzas the poet likens himself or the community to the woman in travail, and to the storm-tossed ship; he is probably describing his personal sufferings and persecutions by the enemies of the sect. The birth of the male child is equivalent to the emergence of the sect itself, and the passage reminds one of the text from Hosea, 11. 1: "When Israel was a child, then I loved him, and called my son out of Egypt".

The author of the poem, the priest-teacher directing the emergent community under duress and opposition, thinks of a ship in heavy water, a woman labouring in child-birth, as the appropriate images for the growing community, or the dying civilization out of which the new is struggling to be reborn. As the Messiah is never mentioned in the poem, and the language is highly metaphorical and imprecise, the Messianic interpretation is one possibility out of three ambiguities but by no means conclusive.

The eschatology of the scrolls is often Messianic by inference, and not by explicit reference. In the War Scroll and the Qumran Hymns or Psalms, the Messiahs are not mentioned. The Rule of the Future Congregation of Israel provides two striking and arresting texts concerning them (I QSa. ii. 11-12, 17-22). "If (God) causes the Anointed One to be born;[7] with them, (the Priest) will come at the head of all the Congregation of Israel, then all his brothers, the Priests the sons of Aaron, then the leaders assembled for the meetings, and they will sit before him, each according to his rank, afterwards will come the Anointed One of Israel". The phrase, "causes the Anointed One to be born", probably looks back to the Old Testament Messianic Psalm 2. 7, and may suggest "divinity by adoption". The second text comes from the passages concerning the sectarian sacred meal. "And [when] they meet together for the common table, to eat and [to drink] new wine, and when the common table shall be prepared for eating and the new wine mixed for drinking, let no one put forth his hand on the first fruits of the bread and the wine before the priest; for he shall bless the first fruits of the bread and wine, and he shall be first [to place] his hand over the bread. Thereafter, the Messiah of Israel shall place his hand over the bread, and all the Congregation of the Community [shall give a] blessing, each one according to precedence in station."

According to this statute shall they proceed at every meal at which at least ten must be gathered together. (I QSa. ii. 17-22).

The meal was celebrated from time to time anticipating the coming of two leaders, the Head Priest, and the "Messiah of Israel", the military leader of the forty years' war, which is to be dated from the death of the Teacher of Righteousness.

"From the day of the death of the one who teaches the Community until the destruction of all the men of war who returned with the 'man of lies' is about forty years" (CD xx (b). 14-15).

Strangely, in the War Scroll, the War is not directed by the Messiah of Israel but by priests. The second edition of the War Scroll was probably published in the final phase of the sect from A.D. 3-68, when in A.D. 68, the monastery was destroyed by Roman soldiers because of the sect's association with, or sympathy for, the Zealot uprisings. The "holy war" of the apocalypse of the Sons of Light and Sons of Darkness is a real war, but it is also an idealistic and transcendental one, with sabbath rests arranged, and angels and demons fighting a spiritual battle in the stratosphere. However, Yahweh, the tribal War God, is the real leader fighting against the "Kittim" (the Romans). His deputy, the Chief Priest (possibly the priestly Messiah of "End-Time") conducts the strategy on his behalf.

There is no rigid pattern of leadership which remains consistent in all the documents throughout the history of the movement. In the Rule for the Future Congregation of Israel the chief priest, the Aaronite titular head of the Community, is to be assisted by the "anointed one of Israel", the military saviour of the sect. The Zadokite Documents probably reveal a change of attitude having arisen in the community, for although the texts describe one leader, the "anointed one of Aaron and Israel", some scholars think that the early texts originally read the "Messiahs". That is quite possible, but it still does not alter the fact that the community of the Zadokite Documents at some stage during the live history of the movement accepted the idea of a priest-warrior in one person. Again, the Rule of the Community explicitly hopes for three leaders: a priest, a soldier and a prophet.

"But they shall be governed by the original rule in which the men of the community were first trained until there arises the prophet and the anointed ones of Aaron and Israel" (I QS. ix. 11). This is the only text, apart from the Messianic testimonia, where the "prophet" is mentioned. A similar imprecision and complexity of type of Messianic leader can be found in the New Testament. At Christ's transfiguration he was associated with Moses and Elijah. Mark 9. 5 "The prophet" of the Fourth Gospel (John 1. 21, and Acts 7. 37) is a Mosaic figure from Deuteronomy, while Melchizedek in Hebrews takes us back to ancient priest-Kings—an interesting complexity of persons all associated by early Christians with the figure of Jesus.

Perhaps the "prophet" came to be identified with one of the Messianic leaders, and a similar liaison may have taken place between the "Teacher of Righteousness" and one of the Messiahs, reducing the triumvirate to two leaders, or eventually two to one. At least one text differentiates the "Righteous Expositor" from the Messiah(s), (CD xx. 1), while two refer to the teacher's peaceful death (CD xx. 1, 14). Some texts point to the founder of the movement, or some famous priest-teacher, as the "Teacher". "And God noticed their deeds, that they sought him with a perfect heart, and he raised up for them a righteous teacher to direct them in his heart's (way)."[8] But the same document also looks for another teacher to lead the movement in the prelude to the Messianic age. ". . . and without them they shall find nothing—until he comes who shall teach righteousness at the coming days" (vi. 11).

The function of the "Teacher of Righteousness", or "Orthodox Teacher", or "Sound Expositor", was to instruct the community in the correct legal interpretations, with special reference to the three stages in the graded novitiate of the sectarian rule. He guided the Council in its deliberations, when it promulgated specific rules for the sabbath, eating, drinking, and bathing, but also in its understanding of the special pesher commentaries on the prophets and other Old Testament texts in the light of the Messianic expectation and the coming "end of days". The expression, "Teacher of Righteousness" is a title; therefore there may have been a number of such teachers. One famous "Teacher", possibly the author of some of the Psalms, made a great impact on the members of the sect. The community hoped for a similar leader, or leaders to invigorate the movement in the "coming days". "Until there shall come he who shall teach righteousness" (CD vi. 11), is one whom the Almighty "will raise up" from the elect community of the living, not from the dead.

The Habakkuk commentary, although it yields seven references to the "Teacher" and several to the "Wicked Priest", has none to the Messianic leaders. Of the many sectarian writings, the Habakkuk commentary is the most eschatological of them all, yet it has no direct reference to the Messianic hope. *If it tarries, wait for it, for it must indeed come, and will not be late.* Interpreted, this concerns the men of truth who do the Law, whose hands shall not tire in their devotion to truth when the last aeon is lengthened. For all the aeons of God attain their appointed end as he determined them in the mysteries of his wisdom" (I QpHab. vii. 9-14).

Something of the spirit of 2 Peter 3. 4, is to be found in this passage i.e. the "last things" may appear to be delayed, but that is no argument against the certainty of them finally coming to take place in the Pompey invasion of 63 B.C.

The Habakkuk commentary has become the most controversial of the scrolls because the texts applied to the "Teacher of Right-eousness" have been interpreted in the sense that the Teacher is the Messianic leader who was crucified and expected to rise from the dead. But God "raising up" a prophet or a leader is not the same as being "raised from the dead"; in addition the sect's belief in the resurrection of the body is unlikely, or at any rate uncertain. Secondly, the Teacher here is a historical person who was perhaps martyred for the movement, although one text speaks of his survival. The circumstances of the persecution and possible death seem to be the sect's unlawful calendar and feast-days.

"Interpreted this concerns the Wicked Priest who pursued the Righteous Teacher to destroy him in the fury of his anger at the place where he discovered him, and at the time of their (fast) Day of Atonement, he appeared to them to cause them to stumble on [their] fast day, their sabbath of rest" (I QpHab. xi. 4-8).

The commentary on Psalm 37, on the contrary, implies that at the moment of trial the Teacher of Righteousness will escape.

"(But God will not desert him into his hand or) let him be condemned when he is tried" (IV QpPs. 37 iv. 7).

However, one Hymn indicates that at some stage of their theology the sectarians were crudely eschatological in their thinking. The Psalmist envisages the fantasy of a literal destruction of the universe by fire, with the creation of a new Heaven and Earth.

The torrents of Belial shall spread to all ends of the mountains.
In all their channels a devouring fire shall destroy every fresh and withered tree on their banks; it shall burn with fiery flames unto the end of all their destructiveness.
It shall devour the foundation of the earth and the dry land.
The foundations of the mountain shall be blasted; the roots of the rocks shall (turn) to torrents of pitch; it shall consume to the depths of the earth (I QH. iii. 29-31).

But this crude eschatology can be cited only from one text, just as the Second Coming of Christ can be quoted from Mark 13 and Revelation in contrast to the transmuted eschatology of the Fourth

Gospel in the doctrine of the "Paraclete". The Qumran Psalmist has made his personal sufferings cosmic. While in the War Scroll the main interest is in the eschatological battle and its outcome, from his Temple Yahweh breathes out in anger a universal physical destruction of the heathen.

> For God shall thunder forth his loud rumblings, and his sacred dwelling shall thunder with the truth of his glory. The heavenly host shall give their thunder and the world's foundations shall stagger and tremble.

> The war of the heavenly warriors shall devour the earth; and it shall not return before the destruction, which shall be endless and indescribable (I QH. iii. 34-36).

Finally, the sect's belief in the future life is certain, but the precise nature of that belief is problematical, both from the texts, and Josephus and Hippolytus.[9] There is no text declaring a final irrevocable judgement for the world by the transcendental "Son of Man" as Judge and/or earthly redeemer. Of great importance in deciding the influence of the sect on Christian origins is the complete absence of this title in all the writings of the Dead Sea Scrolls, in spite of the fact that many chapters from the Enoch writings, excepting chapters 37-71, have been discovered. We search in vain for a text, like Daniel 12. 2, explicitly prophesying the resurrection and judgement of the dead.

> And many of them that sleep in the dust of the earth shall awake, some to everlasting life, and some to shame and everlasting contempt.

The Hymns provide the texts nearest to the idea of resurrection of the flesh.

> And then the Sword of God shall hasten at the time of Judgement, and all the sons of his truth shall arise to [overthrow] the sons of Wickedness. And all the wicked shall be extinct (I QH. vi. 29-30).

> Hoist a flag-staff, you who lie in the dust!
> O worm-like corpses, raise up a banner (I QH. v. 34).

The last two texts may be no more than poetic metaphor, urging the living to fight for the elect, or the pious dead of the past to come to their aid. The following mutilated text, in speaking of the future community who need forgiveness and cleansing, is nearer the Daniel text:

> . . . that worm-like bodies may be raised from the dust to the [eternal] community, and from the perverse spirit to [thy] understanding,

that he may stand before thee with the everlasting host, and with
the spirits [of wisdom],
to be rejuvenated with all the living, and to exult gladly with those
of the community who know thee (I QH. xi. 12-14).

On closer examination, what appears from this text to be the
ultimate destiny of those raised from the dead, is to join the angelic
company of spirits and to be transmuted from the matter into spirit,
from man into angelic being. The Manual and the Angelic Liturgy
support Josephus' assertion that the sect (if Essene) believed in the
immortality of the soul. Hippolytus asserts that they believed in
both the resurrection of the body and the immortality of the soul.

> For they confess that the flesh also will rise and be immortal as the
> soul is already immortal, which they now say, when separated from
> the body, enters a place of fragrant air and light, to rest until the
> judgement . . . for they say there will be a judgement and a con-
> flagration of everything, and that the wicked will be eternally
> punished.[10]

The Angelic Liturgy IV QSl i. 24-26, and the Horoscopes of
Qumran,[11] show that the sect was mystical and dangerously near
to gnosticism in some of its ideas.

> The sixth among the chief Princes will bless [. . .] all the perfect in
> righteous acts with seven words of wonder, so that they should be
> forever with those who live for ever [. . .]
> The seventh of the sovereign Princes shall bless [. . .] who [for
> ever] praise his glorious kingdom with seven wondrous words which
> will be to them for eternal peace.

Such language of the mystical prayer cycle is near to immortality
of the soul and far from real eschatology.

CONCLUSION

To conclude, we may say with confidence that the sect thought
that evil in the present age would increase until the community,
under the inspired guidance of one of their "Orthodox Teachers",
lived the sufficient life of purity essential for God to cause to be
born a Messiah who would conquer the forces of evil in the forty
years' war. A priest of Aaronite line, a true Zadokite, would be
the nominal head of the sect, the Military Messiah, the "Prince of
the Congregational", his assistant and deputy. The teachers of righteousness, the priest-teachers and commentators on the prophets,
would guide and inspire the movement. The immediate outcome of
the struggle would be victory against the Romans and the orthodox
Jewish leaders, with a long period of peace and prosperity. When the
texts describe the future life, they have none of the extreme crudity

of the apocalyptic school. The bliss of the elect as described in the Manual is much nearer to the "immortality of the soul" than to the "resurrection of the flesh". One of the Hymns reflects the cruder eschatology in the idea of total destruction of the universe by fire, but the resurrection from the dead after a final Judgement by the Son of Man is nowhere to be found in the texts. The Angelic Liturgy, a mystical prayer cycle, and the Hymns, are ethereal and Greek in their approach to the world to come, while the Zadokite Documents and the War of the Sons of Light and the Sons of Darkness are preoccupied with this world, with the founding of the community and its struggles for survival.

The Messianic eschatology was developed during the history of the movement, considerable variation in the Messianic ideas being revealed in the texts. The Zadokite Documents mention one Messiah, the Rule of the Community speaks of three leaders, but the Habakkuk commentary, although the most eschatological of all the writings, refers to the martyrdom of the Teacher of Righteousness, but never mentions the Messiahs. In the Future Rule of the Congregation the dual leadership is clearly outlined, but the Hymns, apart from one disputed passage, are not concerned with the Messianic hope, nor on the whole with cruder eschatology.

The relationship of the Teacher of Righteousness to the Messiah is not clear, but perhaps we may infer that he is to be identified with one of the Messianic leaders. In the Zadokite Documents the teacher dies, in the Habakkuk commentary he is martyred, but in Psalm 37 he survives the persecution. The probable answer to the complexity and ambiguity in the texts is that there were several such teachers, but one in particular may have made a great impact on the life of the movement. To assert that he was expected to rise from the dead has no foundation in the texts, but it also presupposes that the sect believed in the resurrection from the dead. On the whole the community's belief in the future life seems to have been transmutation of matter into spirit, or immortality of the soul, with the exception of two of the Hymns which come very near to resurrection.

The main thesis of this essay is to question the conclusion made by the scholars that the sect was thorough-going in its eschatology.[12] A close examination of the texts does not permit us to force into one eschatological pattern the community's beliefs concerning the Messianic hope, the Teacher of Righteousness, and the future life. As with the New Testament, there is no one continuous pattern of uniform doctrine, for the Qumran documents which cover a similar period of over two hundred years oscillate between a this worldly Messianic hope and a near gnostic attitude to the future life.

5

JOHN THE BAPTIST

CHARLES H. H. SCOBIE

OF all the people who appear in the pages of the New Testament none on the face of it seems likely to have had a closer connection with the Qumran sect than John the Baptist.[1]

The Qumran monastery appears to have been restored and re-occupied during the reign of Herod Archelaus (4 B.C.—A.D. 6), so that the sectarians were living there during most of John's lifetime, and certainly during the period of his ministry.

John was born, according to Luke 1. 39, in an unnamed city in the hill country of Judaea; the traditional site of 'Ain Karim is only some twenty miles or so West of Qumran. More significant, how-ever, is the fact that much of John's ministry was conducted in the wilderness of Judaea (Matt. 3. 1), the area lying between the Judaean plateau on the West and the lower stretches of the Jordan and the Dead Sea to the East. While John may have moved around within this region (cf. Luke 3. 3), the main centre of his preaching and baptismal ministry was almost certainly close to the fords of Jordan just South of Jericho, a point less than ten miles North of Qumran. It is impossible to suppose that John could be ignorant of the sectarian settlement existing within the very area in which he himself lived and worked.

To what extent John may have had direct contact with Qumran and whether he was influenced by the sect are questions which are much more difficult to answer. The Scrolls do not mention John or his disciples, and there is no direct evidence of any connection. We can only therefore compare what we know of the Qumran sect with what we know of John and see if the resemblances are close enough to indicate contact and influence.

Josephus devotes one paragraph in his *Antiquities* (XVIII. v. 2) to John the Baptist, a passage which is valuable as far as it goes though it undoubtedly reflects the bias of the author. For our knowledge of John we are therefore almost entirely dependent on the New Testa-

ment. The brief references in the Gospels are not unbiassed themselves, a fact that can be most readily accounted for if, as many
scholars believe, there was a group of John's disciples who formed
a continuing sect after his death, the claims of which the Christian
community had to combat. There is good reason to hold, however,
that the Gospels do preserve early and authentic tradition concerning John, especially in the Q source with its sayings of Jesus
concerning John, and its record of John's preaching.

Josephus and the Gospels agree in testifying to the deep im-
pression John made on the people. This was due primarily to the
message he preached and to the rite of *baptism* which he administered.

John's *message* centres in his proclamation of the imminence of
the judgement and of the Coming One with his twofold baptism of
fire and spirit (Matt. 3. 7-12, Luke 3. 7-17, Mark 1. 4, 7, 8).

The Qumran sect also expected the judgement when the wicked
would be destroyed by *fire* (I QS. ii. 8; 4. 13; I QH. vi. 18; I QpHab.
ii. 11-13; CD ii. 5, 6). One of the Thanksgiving Hymns sheds light on
John's prophecy of an eschatological baptism "with fire", since it
pictures (probably reflecting Iranian influence) a river of fire,

> when the hour of judgement strikes . . .
> when the rivers of Belial
> burst their high banks
> —rivers that are like fire
> devouring all that draw their waters,
> rivers whose runnels destroy
> green tree and dry tree alike,
> rivers that are like fire
> which sweeps like flaming sparks
> devouring all that drink their waters
> —a fire which consumes
> all foundations of clay,
> every solid bedrock;
> when the foundations of the mountains
> become a raging blaze,
> when granite roots are turned
> to streams of pitch,
> when the flame devours
> down to the great abyss,
> when the floods of Belial burst forth
> unto hell itself . . .[2]

Whereas John immersed people in the waters of the Jordan, the
Coming One would immerse the wicked in just such an eschatological river of fire.

Fire is sometimes thought of as a refining and purifying force, destroying what is evil and leaving unharmed what is good. This idea appears e.g. in Mal. 3. 1-3, Prov. 17. 3, 1 Cor. 3. 12-15. It has been suggested that John's prophecy of the Coming One's baptism with fire is to be interpreted in this sense, especially since Mal. 3. 1-3 (linked with Mal. 4. 5, 6) is applied to John in the New Testament (Matt. 11. 10-14).

The evidence we have, however, does not support this contention. John's allusions to a coming baptism of fire reflect the simpler idea of fire as a means of punishment or destruction of the wicked. It is the tree that does not bear good fruit that is cut down and thrown into the fire (Matt. 3. 10, Luke 3. 9), and it is only after the wheat has been gathered into the granary that the chaff is burned (Matt. 3. 12, Luke 3. 17).

The Scrolls certainly contain references to trial and testing (e.g. I QS. i. 17, iv. 20-22, viii. 4; I QM. xvii. 1, 9; CD xx. 27), but fire is not mentioned in these passages. On the other hand, in the passages referred to above where the Scrolls speak of the eschatological fire, the idea is generally not that of testing or refining but, as in the case of John's preaching, of the punishment or destruction of the wicked.

John also prophesied a future baptism with *holy spirit* (Matt. 3. 11 Luke 3. 16, Mark 1. 18). While the New Testament writers obviously regard John as foretelling the giving of "the Holy Spirit" in the full Christian sense, there is no need to reject the reference to the spirit as a later Christian addition to John's message. An eschatological outpouring of God's spirit was a familiar part of Jewish expectation (Isa. 32. 15, Ezek. 39. 29, Joel 2. 28, 29), and the actual phrase "holy spirit" (as in John's preaching, without capitals or definite article) occurs in the Old Testament, as also in the Scrolls (e.g. I QS. viii. 16, I QH. vii. 6, CD ii. 12). There is nothing at all impossible in the view that John did indeed proclaim a future outpouring of God's spirit.

But why should this be referred to as *baptism* with holy spirit? Already in the Old Testament the gift of the spirit is compared to the pouring out of water (e.g. in Isa. 44. 3), and in Ezek. 36. 25-27 the future gift of the spirit is linked with sprinkled water—"I will sprinkle clean water upon you, and you shall be clean from your uncleannesses, and from all your idols I will cleanse you. A new heart will I give you, and a new spirit I will put within you . . ."

The Scrolls, however, provide a particularly close parallel in I QS. iv. 20, 21. "God will refine in his truth all the deeds of man, and will purify for himself the frame of man, consuming every spirit of error hidden in his flesh, and cleansing him *with holy spirit* from all wicked deeds. And he will sprinkle on him a spirit of truth like water for impurity." The interpretation of this passage has been much disputed, but most probably it refers to God's elect (i.e. the Qumran sect themselves) upon whom, at the last day, God will pour out his holy spirit. This future outpouring of holy spirit is spoken of in terms used elsewhere of the sect's baptismal rites ("water for impurity").

Several writers wish to *identify* the fire and the spirit of John's message, regarding them as referring to essentially one and the same cleansing, purging, refining power. On this view all men will be baptized by fire/spirit; the wicked will not survive the test but will be destroyed, whereas God's elect will emerge cleansed and purified. We have already urged above, however, that the evidence shows that John foretold an outpouring of fire only on the wicked, who would thus be punished or destroyed. The evidence of the Scrolls (as also of the Old Testament) suggests likewise that it is only on the elect that spirit will be poured out. Thus John proclaims *two* baptisms, not one.

On the other hand, the holy spirit which is poured out on the elect is, according to I QS. iv. 20, 21, in part at least a purifying force which will cleanse a man's body and spirit from whatever impurity remains. It will also confer on a man knowledge, wisdom, and strength.

The Scrolls therefore help us to see how John proclaimed a future twofold baptism, of the wicked with fire, and of the elect with holy spirit, and they help us to understand how John probably interpreted these ideas.

In John's preaching these future baptisms will be administered by one who is to come after John and who is mightier than he (Mark 1. 7 etc.), evidently a messianic figure of some kind. (Josephus betrays his bias by failing to mention John's messianic preaching at all.)

If the Qumran sect, at one stage at least, expected the coming of *two* Messiahs, one kingly and one priestly, then John's expectation differed from this, for he proclaimed a single figure, the Coming One (cf. Luke 7. 19, Matt. 11. 3). Nor does this Coming One have much in common with those passages in the Scrolls which lend support to the traditional Davidic Warrior Messiah (cf. e.g. I QSb. v. 20-28). The elaborate eschatological timetable of the War Scroll is even further from John's thought, which is always simple, clear, and direct. If the Coming One is primarily an apocalyptic, supernatural judge then the closest parallel is to the expectation of the Son of Man, a figure who does *not* appear in the Scrolls. On the other hand, the saying about untying (or carrying) the Coming One's sandals (Mark 1. 7, Matt. 3. 11, Luke 3. 16), as also John's question from prison (Luke

7. 9, Matt. 11. 3), suggest an earthly figure, possibly one as yet un-recognized, who will be exalted to heaven as Son of Man.

At any rate, as regards his messianic preaching John does not appear to have had any special links with Qumran. It may well be that in this area John was deliberately vague, not wishing to identify himself with any particular branch of messianic expectation, but preferring to use the most general title available, "The Coming One".

Both Josephus and the New Testament ascribe to John the nickname "The Baptist", and indicate that his rite of *baptism* played a prominent part in his ministry. "John was a pious man," Josephus tells us, "and he was bidding the Jews who practised virtue and exercised righteousness toward each other and piety toward God to come together for baptism. For thus it seemed to him would baptismal ablution be acceptable if it were used, not to beg off from sins committed but for the purification of the body when the soul had previously been cleansed by righteous conduct" (*Antiq.* XVIII. v. 2). Josephus seems to think of John's baptism in terms of the ritual and ceremonial lustrations "for the purification of the body" which were required by the Law (Lev. 11—15, Numbers 19) and which were considerably developed and extended in the post-Old Testament period. John, as a pious Jew, would no doubt have observed the laws of ritual purity, but his own baptism, which he administered, which caused such a wide stir and which earned him his nickname, was obviously something different from the usual Jewish rites.

The Gospels give us more reliable information at this point with their reference to John's "baptism of repentance for the forgiveness of sins" (Mark 1. 4), and especially their linking of John's baptism with his eschatological proclamation (Luke 3. 16, Matt. 3. 11).

John's rite has often been connected with that of Jewish proselyte baptism, but this view involves serious difficulties. The evidence for proselyte baptism prior to A.D. 70 is very slight, and there are obvious differences between it and John's baptism. The Dead Sea Scrolls have raised the question as to whether John's closest affinities in this regard were not with the sectarian, baptist move-ment.

The Scrolls sect emphasized baptismal rites,[3] probably extensions of the Old Testament ritual and ceremonial washings. We are reminded of Josephus' comments on the regular washings of the Essenes (*B.J.* II. viii. 5; cf. also *B.J.* II. viii. 3 and 10). Special sig-nificance, however, attaches to the sections in the Manual of Discipline which deal with *entry* into the sect. New members were admitted and the community as a whole participated in a solemn ceremony of renewal of the covenant once a year, almost certainly at the Feast of Weeks or Pentecost. Although the Manual gives part of the liturgy used on this occasion (see I QS. 1. 16—3. 12), and comments on its meaning and significance, unfortunately it does not describe the rites or ceremonies involved.

Candidates for membership were required to make *confession* of their sin in the following terms: "We have commited iniquity, we have transgressed, we have sinned, we have done evil, we and our fathers before us, in walking contrary to the statutes of truth; but righteous is God, and true is his judgement on us and on our fathers; and the mercy of his steadfast love he has bestowed upon us from everlasting to everlasting" (I QS. i. 24—ii. 1).

The section I QS. ii. 25f takes up the theme of those who refuse to enter the covenant, possibly with special reference to those who have undergone the probationary period but who refuse to become full members. Of such a person it is said that

> He will not be purified by atonement offerings,
>   and he will not be made clean with water for impurity.
> He will not sanctify himself with seas and rivers,
>   or be made clean with any water for washing.
> Unclean, unclean will he be all the days that he rejects the ordinances
>   of God, not being instructed in the community of his counsel.

The implication is that the man who does enter the community is washed and cleansed from uncleanness. Similarly, I QS. v. 7-20 also deals with entry into the community, warning that the wicked "shall not enter the water, in order to touch the sacred food of the holy men, for they will not be cleansed unless they have turned from their evil". Here, becoming a member of the community is equated with entering the water and being cleansed. One recalls Josephus' comment that the candidate for membership of the Essenes, after his first probationary year "is brought into closer touch with the rule and is allowed to share the purer kind of holy water" (*B.J.* II. viii. 7). To many scholars this has suggested some kind of baptism of initiation and certainly the references to washing with water in the context of entry into the sect are highly significant.

One of the most striking features of the references to entering the covenant and to the rites of baptism is the emphasis on the need for *confession* and *repentance*. The sect called themselves "the penitents of Israel" (CD vi. 5, viii. 16), and the formula of confession on entering the covenant was quoted above. I QS. v. 14 stresses the fact that the wicked "will not be cleansed unless they have turned from their evil". Clearly, the cleansing conferred by baptism is conditional on repentance.

The various rites of washing in Judaism were intended to cleanse only from ritual or ceremonial defilement; they did not apply to the uncleanness of *moral* failure. Of course, the prophets called the people to repent of their moral failings, and promised God's forgiveness conditional on this repentance—"Let the wicked forsake his way, and the unrighteous man his thoughts, let him return to the Lord, that he may have mercy upon him, and to our God, for he will abundantly pardon" (Isa. 55. 7). Cleansing from sin in this sense, however, was not associated with any rites of washing. What we find in the Scrolls then is a drawing together of these two ideas. Moral offences render a man ritually unclean and therefore require rites of ablution. No washings on the other hand are of any avail without sincere repentance.

This certainly calls to mind John's "baptism of repentance for the forgiveness of sins". John's demand that men repent—turn from evil and turn to God—before coming to baptism, and his demand that after baptism the sincerity of their repentance should be demonstrated by good works, would have been completely endorsed by the Scrolls sect. We must note, however, that in John the concern for ritual cleanness, so pronounced in the sect, passes into the background and the emphasis is now firmly upon moral obedience to the will of God. John seems to have carried the tendency of the Scrolls sect further by linking an actual rite of washing with his appeal for repentance and promise of God's forgiveness. One feels that John must have been strongly influenced here by passages in the prophets which use the figure of cleansing (e.g. Isa. 1. 16-18).

John's baptism also recalls ideas found in the Scrolls in its *eschatological* emphasis, for John, like the sectarians, expected the imminent approach of the new age. Those who submitted to John's baptism did not need to fear the river of fire which would be poured out on the wicked; they would enjoy the blessing of God's holy spirit. So the Qumran sectarians, through initiation into the sect, separated themselves from those whom God would destroy by fire; and already they experienced to some extent the cleansing and sanctification of God's spirit which would be experienced in its fulness at the end of days. This is seen from I QS. iii. 7-9 which says of the man who enters the sect,

> in a holy spirit he will be united in his truth,
> and he will be cleansed from all his iniquities;
> and in an upright and humble spirit his sin will be atoned,
> and in the submission of his soul to all the statutes of God,
>   his flesh will be cleansed;
> that he may be sprinkled with water for impurity,
> and sanctify himself with water of cleanness.

This recalls the passage I QS. iv. 20, 21 (above, p. 61) where the eschatological cleansing by holy spirit is referred to in similar terms, and is also linked with the idea of sprinkling with water under the influence of Ezek. 36. 25.

Initiation into the Qumran sect marked entry into the *covenant*, that is into the true Israel. Although those entering the sect were all Jews, merely being born a Jew no longer constituted membership in the people of God. Israel as a whole had rejected and disobeyed God, and thus it was that the sectarians felt called through repentance and dedication to the Law to enter into a new covenant with God, the new covenant foretold by Jeremiah (Jer. 31. 31-34, cf. CD viii. 21, xx. 12). They formed the new Israel, existing at the present time in the "dominion of Belial" but soon to enjoy all the blessings promised to God's people in the new age.

John also restricted his ministry to Jews, and he believed that descent from Abraham was not by itself enough (Luke 3. 8, Matt. 3. 9). In view of the imminent approach of the Coming One John too sought to prepare God's people for the new age. Although our information regarding John's baptism is meagre, the Scrolls suggest that baptism marked entry into the eschatological community. Here we must carefully note, however, that our sources give no indication that John's baptism granted admission into a sect or a monastic community. John apparently gathered a group of disciples round him, but the great majority of those baptized returned to their daily occupations (Luke 3. 10-14).

This fact points up another contrast between John and Qumran. Though the sectarians probably had some kind of baptism of initiation, their primary emphasis was on the regular, repeated washings which formed an important part of the life of the sect. On the other hand, John's "baptism", for which he was famous, appears (so far as we can gather) to have been a non-repeatable rite. This does not mean that John did not practise regular washings of the traditional type also; John 3. 25 appears to be an isolated fragment which suggests his interest in matters of ritual purity.[4] The difference is rather one of emphasis, John laying all the stress on the need for a once-for-all decision, for a clean break with sin, for a life befitting a member of the true people of God, and symbolizing this therefore by the once-for-all rite of baptism.

Turning to some other features of John's ministry, his *asceticism* suggests links with the Qumran sect and the sectarian movement in general. He made do with a meagre diet of "locusts and wild honey" (Mark 1. 6), and came "eating no bread and drinking no wine" (Luke 7. 33). John and his disciples practised fasting, in contrast to

the example of Jesus and his disciples (Mark 2. 18f and parallels; cf.
Matt. 11. 18, 19).

A passage on food laws in the Damascus Document (CD xii.
12-15) deals with three kinds of food, honey, fish, and locusts, so
that evidently John's diet was typical of the Scrolls sect also. Philo
indicates that honey was part of the frugal diet of the Essenes when
he mentions that "some superintend the swarms of bees" (*Hypothetica* IX. 11. 8). This means nothing more, however, than that
these foods were typical of the general area in which both John
and the Essenes lived.

If Luke 7. 33 is to be taken quite literally to mean that bread and
wine were excluded from John's diet, then his asceticism would
appear to have been more severe than that of the Qumran sectarians,
since a feature of their life was common meals at which bread and
wine were consumed after being blessed by a priest (I QS. vi. 4-6).

It has been noted that the word for "wine" in the Scrolls is not
the usual term *yayin*, but *tīrōsh*. While *tīrōsh* is occasionally used as
the equivalent of *yayin*, i.e. as meaning fermented wine capable of
producing intoxication if taken in excess, it properly refers to the
freshly pressed and still unfermented juice of the grape, technically
known as "must". It may well be therefore that Milik is right in
suggesting that in the Scrolls *tīrōsh* is not wine in the normal sense
but means " 'sweet wine', a wine only lightly fermented to prevent
it from going bad". Leaney translates *tīrōsh* as "grape juice".[5]
Josephus refers to the "invariable sobriety" of the Essenes (B.J. II,
viii, 5), a comment which might imply abstinence from fully fermented wine. On the other hand, it is possible that *tīrōsh* is used
in the Scrolls as a poetic archaism, and that the sobriety of the
Essenes referred to by Josephus was due simply to an invariable
moderation, "the limitations of the allotted portions of meat and
drink to the demands of nature" (*B.J.* II. viii. 5).

The Scrolls indicate beyond doubt that the sect ate bread, and
one of the buildings at Qumran has been identified as a bakery.
Josephus describes how, at the common meals of the Essenes "the
baker serves out the loaves to them in order" (*B.J.* II. viii. 5). Moreover, archaeological evidence indicates that meat was consumed
at Qumran, while investigations at 'Ain Feshka suggest a kind of
"home farm" operated by the community.

The probability is therefore that John's asceticism was more
severe than that of the Qumran sect. John does not appear to have
been a member of a monastic community, certainly not of the
type pictured by Philo in his description of the Essenes who labour
all day in the fields and share the products of their toil (*Hypothetica*
IX. 11. 8f.; cf. Josephus, *B.J.* II. viii. 5 and *Antiq.* XVIII. i. 5).

John's diet may in part be accounted for by the fact that his other activities left him no time to obtain a more adequate sustenance than the locusts and wild honey of the wilderness which could be gathered without cultivation.

Undoubtedly, however, John's asceticism is to be understood primarily in the light of the common Jewish understanding of fasting as an expression of humiliation before God and of repentance for sin (cf. Jonah 3. 5, Ecclesiasticus 34. 26). By his fasting, John was demonstrating in his own life the repentance and humility before God which he demanded in his preaching.

Many writers have seen a close connection between John and the Scrolls sect on the grounds that in both cases their location in the *wilderness* was based on an interpretation of Isa. 40. 3. The Qumran community (or perhaps a smaller, original, pioneer group which paved the way for the later community) quoted this verse in the following context: "When these things shall come to pass for the community in Israel, by these regulations they shall be separated from the midst of the session of the men of error to go to the wilderness to prepare there the way of the Lord; as it is written, 'in the wilderness prepare the way of the Lord; make straight in the desert a highway for our God.' This is the study of the Law, as he commanded through Moses, to do according to all that has been revealed by his holy spirit" (I QS. viii. 12-16; cf. ix. 19, 20). This same text is quoted in the Gospels in connection with John's wilderness ministry (Mark 1. 3, Matt. 3. 3, Luke 3. 4, John 1. 23).

Undoubtedly both John and the Qumran sect were influenced by the rich complex of historical and eschatological associations which had gathered around the term "the wilderness". There is, however, a quite significant difference in the interpretation of Isa. 40. 3. In the Manual of Discipline, the introductory phrase "a voice cries" is omitted, and the original parallelism is retained:

"In the wilderness prepare the way of the Lord,
Make straight in the desert a highway for our God."

This preparation is interpreted as the study and practice of the scriptures, especially of the Torah.

The New Testament references to Isa. 40. 3, on the other hand, all quote the introductory words, taking them with the first phrase of what follows so that the parallelism is broken: *"The voice of one crying in the wilderness, Prepare the way of the Lord, make his paths straight."* The emphasis is on the voice crying in the wilderness, because John was primarily a *preacher*, whose voice and whose call for repentance was heard by the crowds. The Qumran sect's withdrawal to the wilderness was motivated by a desire for separation "from the midst of the session of the men of error".

Separation is a major theme in the Scrolls; only by withdrawing from wicked and apostate Israel can the sect truly study and apply the Law and keep themselves pure and holy. John's motivation, on the other hand, was entirely different. While remaining within the area of the wilderness, his location at the fords of Jordan, where different travel routes converged, allowed him to have contact with apostate Israel and to preach his message to large numbers of people.

In view of the significance of the wilderness for the Qumran (and other) groups, it is clearly quite unnecessary to suggest, as some form critics have done, that John's wilderness ministry is a later invention, a Christian formulation making him fulfil the prophecy of Isa. 40. 3.[6] That John ministered in the wilderness can be taken as certain; that he was influenced in this by Isa. 40. 3 is very probable. Whether John actually quoted the text himself, however, is not quite so clear, since none of the Synoptics place it on John's own lips. On the other hand, the evidence of the Scrolls does raise the question as to whether in this instance, the Fourth Gospel may not preserve the more accurate tradition.[7]

John's *priestly descent* (Luke 1. 5) has also been urged as a link with the Qumran sect which had a strong priestly emphasis. But so far as we know, priestly ideas played no part in John's thought, and in any case his father Zechariah served in the Jerusalem Temple whereas the Scrolls sect had severed all connection with the official Temple cult.

It will now be apparent that there are close resemblances between John and the Qumran sect, and that at several points the Scrolls have shed valuable light on John's preaching and practices. We have also noted, however, a number of important differences. Certainly as we meet him in our sources John is not a member of a sect or a monastic community, at Qumran or anywhere else. He is an individual and original figure, subject only to God. His most important difference from the Qumran group lies in his refusal to separate completely from apostate Israel, and in his mission of preaching and baptism directed to the people. His message was much more genuinely prophetic than that of the Scrolls group, and it was also characterized by a force and a simplicity not found in the Scrolls.

Some have sought to explain this relationship of resemblance and difference by suggesting that John was adopted by the Qumran sect, interpreting Luke 1. 80 ("and the child grew and became strong in spirit, and he was in the wilderness till the day of his manifestation to Israel") in the light of Josephus' comment that the Essenes adopt young children and train them up (*B.J.* II. viii. 2). The Rule of the Congregation gives directions for the training of boys from the age of ten upwards (I QSa. i. 8). Others have suggested that John may have served the probationary period in the sect, but refused full membership.

With such suggestions we enter the realm of speculation. It is much safer to suggest that the Scrolls support the view which sees John in the context of a number of roughly similar groups active in the Jordan valley area and making up a non-conformist, baptist, sectarian movement within the Judaism of the period. This movement forms the background of John's ministry, and undoubtedly influenced his thought at many points. It is from this movement that John emerges as an independent and individual figure with a highly distinctive message of his own, a message which in its simplicity and prophetic urgency, in its call for repentance and cleansing, in its confident proclamation of a new age about to dawn was used, in the providence of God, as the starting point for the mission and ministry of the historical Jesus.

6

JESUS AND THE GOSPELS
IN THE LIGHT OF THE SCROLLS

F. F. BRUCE

IN any comparison of the Qumran literature with the Gospels there is an initial difficulty to be taken into account: the historical subject-matter of the Gospels is far more securely established than that of the Qumran literature. For example, whatever doubt may be entertained of other elements in the story of Jesus, the fact that he was crucified by sentence of Pontius Pilate fixes his position in history within narrow limits, for Pilate was prefect of Judaea from A.D. 26 to 36/37. If it were possible to fix the death of the Qumran Teacher of Righteousness within ten or twelve years, we should count ourselves fortunate indeed. As it is, two of the most distinguished British scholars who have dealt with this subject assign to the death of the Teacher dates separated from each other by over 230 years: H. H. Rowley identifies him with the high priest Onias III, who was assassinated in 171 B.C., while G. R. Driver identifies him with the Zealot leader Menahem, who was killed in September, A.D. 66. It must make a difference to a comparative study of Qumran and the Gospels whether we date the Teacher of Righteousness before Christ or after Christ. But even G. R. Driver, while maintaining the post-Christian dating of the Scrolls, insists that "they are documents of prime importance for the understanding of the New Testament and present a challenge which Christian scholars will neglect at their peril" (*The Judaean Scrolls*, 1965, p. 6). His words are still more to be heeded if, as is assumed for purposes of this essay, both the Teacher of Righteousness and the bulk of the Qumran texts thus far published are pre-Christian.

FULFILMENT OF PROPHECY

According to Mark, the burden of Jesus' early Galilean preaching was: "The time is fulfilled, and the kingdom of God is at hand;

repent, and believe in the gospel" (Mark 1. 15). According to Luke, he then began to announce the good news which an unnamed speaker in Isa. 61. 1 (probably to be identified with the Servant of Isa. 42—53) is anointed to proclaim. Thus he served notice that the time appointed for the accomplishment of God's promises to Israel had arrived; that the everlasting kingdom of the God of heaven, foreseen in the visions of Daniel, was about to be set up—indeed, that it was in a sense already present in his own words and deeds. This eschatological emphasis is perhaps the most outstanding feature common to the Gospels and the Qumran literature. According to the Zadokite work, the Teacher of Righteousness was raised up by God to "make known to the last generations what he was about to do in the last generation" (CD i. 12). According to the Habakkuk commentary, it was to the Teacher of Righteousness that "God made known all the mysteries of the words of his servants the prophets" (I QpHab. vii. 4f.). Thanks to the Teacher's insight and instruction, the men of Qumran knew themselves to be living in the last days of the current age, the "epoch of wickedness", and saw it as their duty to prepare the way of the Lord for the new age which was about to dawn.

Let it be said here that the Jesus with whom this essay is concerned is the Jesus of the Gospels. No attempt will be made to draw a distinction between the Jesus of history and the kerygmatic Jesus of post-Easter faith, any more than one will (or could) be made to distinguish the historical Teacher of Righteousness from the Teacher as he appears in the Qumran texts.

In the Qumran texts and in the Gospels the Hebrew prophets are valued and interpreted in their own right; they are not relegated (as so often in rabbinical Judaism) to the role of providing comments or *haphtaroth* to the Torah. In the Qumran literature those covenant-breakers are denounced "who will not believe when they hear all that is coming upon the last generation, from the mouth of the priest [presumably the Teacher of Righteousness] into whose heart God has put wisdom, to interpret all the words of his servants the prophets, through whom God told all that was to come upon his people and upon his land" (I QpHab. ii. 6-10); similarly Jesus chides his disciples, calling them "foolish men" because they were so "slow of heart to believe all that the prophets have spoken" (Luke 24. 25). The time at which the prophetic oracles would be fulfilled was not made known to the prophets themselves; it was revealed to the Teacher of Righteousness, and communicated by him to his disciples, who thus had reason to thank God for divulging to them his "wonderful mysteries" which were concealed from others. So Jesus thanks God for revealing to babes things that had been hidden from the wise and understanding (Matt. 11. 25; Luke 10. 21) and congratulates his hearers because they see and hear things that prophets and righteous men longed in vain to see and hear (Matt. 13. 16f.; Luke 10. 23f.). The distinctive theology of each of the two bodies of literature is based in great measure on the interpretation of prophecy characteristic of each.

In the Qumran literature, however, there is a note of hope deferred which is absent from the Gospels. It may be that at one time the winding up of the old age was expected within the life-time of the Teacher of Righteousness, but its postponement beyond his death called for some reinterpretation of prophecy: "the last time is prolonged, extending beyond all that the prophets have spoken, for the mysteries of God are wonderful" (I QpHab. vii. 7f.). This reminds us of the New Testament problem of the postponement of the parousia, but while this problem has left its mark here and there in the Gospels (cf. Luke 19. 11; John 21. 22f.) their dominant theme is that the age of fulfilment is here. "Today this scripture has been fulfilled in your hearing", says Jesus in the Nazareth synagogue after reading Isa. 61. 1f. (Luke 4. 21); his contemporaries should understand that his casting out demons is a sign that the kingdom of God has arrived (Matt. 12. 28; Luke 11. 20), and if it has not yet arrived "with power", it will do so very soon (Mark 9. 1); the limitations under which he labours at present will disappear once he has undergone his coming baptism (Luke 12. 50)—a baptism which, in the light of Mark 10. 38f., can readily be identified with his death. There is a difference here which is bound up with the differing roles ascribed to Jesus and the Teacher of Righteousness by their respective disciples.

INTERPRETATION OF LAW

In their understanding and application of the Torah, Jesus and the Qumran community differ from contemporary schools of Jewish thought (including the various Pharisaic schools), but they diverge radically the one from the other. A superficial resemblance has indeed been recognized in their respective interpretations of the marriage law. The words of Gen. 1. 27 are quoted as authoritative by Jesus in the form "from the beginning of creation 'God made them male and female'" (Mark 10. 6) and in the Qumran literature in the form "the foundation of creation is: 'male and female he created them'" (CD iv. 21)—but Jesus combines these words with Gen. 2. 24 to prove that marriage is lifelong and divorce forbidden, whereas the Zadokite work combines them with Gen. 7. 9 to prove that a man should not have two wives simultaneously. Divorce was not forbidden at Qumran: there is a mutilated passage in the Zadokite laws which seems to provide that a man proposing to divorce his wife must first get the permission of the overseer (*mebaqqer*) of his "camp" (CD xiii. 17), and in any case Jesus' appeal from the divorce law of Deut. 24. 1-4 to the original purpose of the marriage institution would not have accorded with the Qumran outlook.

The divergence is even more marked in the interpretation of the sabbath law, where Jesus again appeals to the original intention of the institution. If Pharisaic interpretations of the law which conflicted with its original intention incurred Jesus' displeasure, we may readily imagine what he would have said of the still stricter interpretations of the Qumran community. Jesus assumes that all shades of Pharisaic opinion will agree with him that a domestic animal which falls into a pit on the sabbath must be rescued, for all the sacredness of the day (Matt. 12. 11; Luke 14. 5), but precisely such a humane action is forbidden in the Zadokite laws: "Let no man assist a beast in birth on the sabbath day; even if she drops [her young] into a cistern or pit, let him not lift it up on the sabbath" (CD xi. 13f.).

Not only in their detailed interpretation of the law, but in their general separatism, the Qumran community showed a strictness exceeding that of the Pharisees. The Pharisees were concerned about holiness and purity, but did not go out to the wilderness to avoid contamination nor did they take nothing to do with the temple services, much as they disapproved of the temple authorities. In the eyes of the men of Qumran, the Pharisees were half-hearted in the zeal for separation, "seekers after smooth things" (or "givers of smooth interpretations"), as they are repeatedly called in the Qumran texts. If Jesus was criticized by the Pharisees for the laxity of his legal observance and social habits, he would have incurred much fiercer criticism from the men of Qumran, who criticized the Pharisees themselves in this respect.

The First Evangelist says that Jesus described the Pharisees as a "plant which my heavenly Father has not planted" (Matt. 15. 13), a form of words reminiscent of the Qumran community's self-description as "a cultivated root which God caused to sprout . . . to possess his land and grow fat in the goodness of his soil" (CD i. 7f.), a sprout sent out by God "as a flower that will bloom for ever" (I QH. vi. 15). Other strictures of his upon them are found in all the Gospels. Among his recorded sayings, on the other hand, there is no express reference to the men of Qumran or to the Essenes (the relation between these, if there was any, is not our present concern). There may, however, be implicit references, and critical ones at that. W. D. Davies has suggested that the Sermon on the Mount "reveals an awareness of the Sect and perhaps a polemic against it" (*The Setting of the Sermon on the Mount*, 1964, p. 235)—a polemic which was later edited so as to find a new target in the rabbis of Jamnia.

Jesus' correction of the old-time saying, "You shall love your neighbour and hate your enemy" (Matt. 5. 43), would certainly be applicable to a Qumran attitude, whether Qumran was uppermost in his mind or not. For it is laid down among the duties of the initiate into the covenant-community that "he shall love all the sons of light, each according to his lot, in the council of God and hate all the sons of darkness, each according to his guilt, in the vengeance of God" (I QS. i. 9-11; cf. Josephus, *B.J.* II. viii. 7). True, there was nothing personal or self-regarding in this holy hatred, but it connotes something more positive than the "lesser love" which the term occasionally connotes on the lips of Jesus (Luke 14. 26). A member of the Qumran community was forbidden to kill a Gentile for such an unworthy motive as material gain (CD xii. 6f.), but he was not commanded to do him good or voluntarily go a second mile to help him.

HEALING AND THE HOLY SPIRIT

As for Jesus' healing ministry, a parallel to the repeated Gospel acts of healing through the laying on of hands has been pointed out by David Flusser (*I.E.J.* 7, 1957, pp. 107f.) in the Genesis Apocryphon, where Abraham relieves Pharaoh of the evil spirit which brought sickness on him by laying his hands on him (I Q Gen. Apoc. x. 21f., 29). When more material from Cave 4 has been published, further Qumran parallels to the healing narratives in the Gospels will no doubt be recognized. We recall Josephus's testimony to the Essenes' proficiency in the healing art (*B.J.* II. viii. 6) and the opinion of some modern scholars that the word "Essene" is derived from the Aramaic participle *'āsē, 'āsyā*, meaning "healer".

There is not in the teaching of Jesus the same predestinated cleavage between the good and the wicked as is stated in the Qumran Rule, where men are divided between the spirits of truth and perversity until the day of divine visitation (I QS. iii. 18ff.). The closest Gospel affinities with this teaching are found in the Fourth Gospel. But in the Synoptic records Jesus' successful campaign against the demons—emissaries of the realm of darkness—that afflict human beings is carried on by the power of the Spirit of God (Matt. 12. 28), and therefore to attribute his activity to demonic power is to be guilty of blasphemy against the Holy

Spirit (Mark 3. 22-30). John the Baptist's prediction that the Coming One would baptize with the Holy Spirit (Mark 1. 8) thus began to be fulfilled in the ministry of Jesus; in his ministry the age of the Spirit (like the kingdom of God) was being inaugurated. The Qumran community also thought of the age to come as the age of the Spirit; indeed, the establishment of their community and its way of holiness, they believed, provided a foundation for the Holy Spirit (I QS. ix. 3).

COMMUNITY ORGANIZATION

If the Teacher of Righteousness was not the absolute founder of the Qumran community, he was its organizer. It was organized as a miniature Israel, for he envisaged it as the righteous remnant of Israel, the true covenant-community; particular care was taken, too, to preserve the priestly and levitical orders within the wider community. Unnecessary doubt has been cast on Jesus' intention to found a community. That his disciples formed a self-conscious community is clear, and that he himself envisaged them as the true Israel of the end-time is suggested by his selection of twelve of them to play a special role both immediately, as his close companions, and in the new age, when they would "sit on twelve thrones, judging the twelve tribes of Israel" (Matt. 19. 28; cf. Luke 22. 30). The general body of his disciples was the "little flock" for which the Father, in his good pleasure, had designed the kingdom (Luke 12. 32).

The twelve selected by Jesus have been compared with the twelve men who, together with (rather than including) three priests, formed a basis for the establishment of the Qumran community (I QS. viii. 1). These fifteen men at Qumran have commonly been envisaged as an inner council, but perhaps those commentators are right who understand them as the nucleus with which the Teacher of Righteousness began when he set himself to organize the community. The twelve laymen probably represent the twelve lay tribes of Israel (and to this extent are parallel to the twelve apostles of Jesus), while the three priests would represent the three families (Gershon, Kohath, and Merari) of the tribe of Levi. The priestly and levitical elements in the community appear to have received representation beyond their numerical strength; this is bound up with the general priestly emphasis in its organization (each group of ten, for example, into which the community was divided for various purposes, was to include at least one priest). No such priestly or levitical emphasis appears in the Gospels; the principal followers of Jesus were laymen, like Jesus himself. If in due course an attempt was made to establish a new priesthood in the family of Jesus (James the Just and his relatives), this was a later development and unknown to the Gospels.

The rock on which Jesus proposed to build his Church (Matt. 16. 18) may be compared with the description of the covenant-community as "the tried wall, the precious corner-stone, whose foundations will not tremble nor flee from their place" (I QS. viii. 7f.), or a plantation whose "roots strike down into the flinty rock, to secure its stock in earth" (I QH. viii. 23).

The covenant-community built on this sure foundation is a living temple: "a holy place for Israel and the secret council (or foundation) of a holy of holies for Aaron" (I QS. viii. 5f.)—"Israel" being the laity and "Aaron" being the priesthood. When Jesus was examined before the high priest he was accused of saying, "I will destroy this temple that is made with hands, and in three days I will build another, not made with hands" (Mark 14. 58); and this theme of a temple not made with hands is embedded in the general New Testament teaching about the new people of God constituted by Jesus through his death and resurrection. But here, unlike the Qumran situation, no distinction is made between the holy place and the holy of holies; the distinction between priesthood and laity is unknown in the earliest Christian community, for the whole community (non-levitical though it is) bears a priestly character.

Some of the followers of Jesus made greater sacrifices than others. Peter speaks of himself and his colleagues as having "left everything" to follow him (Mark 10. 28). True, they did not have to isolate themselves in the wilderness, or subject themselves to such rigid asceticism as marked John the Baptist. If Jesus "came eating and drinking" and was reproached as "a glutton and a drunkard, a friend of tax collectors and sinners" (Matt. 11. 19; Luke 7. 34), he presented a contrast not only to John, who came "eating no bread and drinking no wine" (Luke 7. 33), but to the austere men of Qumran. Yet to follow him closely meant leaving house, brothers, sisters, mother, father, children, and lands for his sake and for the gospel (Mark 10. 29). It is debatable how far the men of Qumran had to give up family life, but it is difficult to imagine how it could have been enjoyed in anything like a normal fashion in their wilderness retreat. Some burials of women and children have indeed been identified in the Qumran cemetery, and marriage and family life are contemplated in the Zadokite work and in the Rule of the Congregation (I QSa). There may have been changes in this regard in the two centuries of the community's life; in any case, we probably have to distinguish between those who embraced the full rigours of coenobitic life in the wilderness and those who remained at home as well-wishers and possibly "associate members", whose hospitality would always be available to full members if ever they found it necessary to travel abroad. Jesus' reference to some who had "made themselves eunuchs for the sake of the kingdom of heaven" (Matt. 19. 12) would be applicable to certain members of the Qumran community as well as of his own following. When the twelve, sent out to preach two by two, were told to find out who was "worthy" in any town or village they entered (Matt. 10. 11), the reference is probably to people who, like Joseph of Arimathaea, were known to be "looking for the kingdom of God" (Mark 15. 43; cf. Luke 2. 25, 38) and might be expected to sympathize with the mission of Jesus and the twelve to the point of providing them with free hospitality.

It is plain that during Jesus' ministry he and his disciples were dependent on such private generosity; some well-to-do women who "provided for them out of their means" are mentioned in Luke 8. 2f. They shared a common purse, and Judas Iscariot is named as their treasurer (John 12. 6; 13. 29). But nothing like the carefully regulated administration of the Qumran common fund was required at this stage of the disciples' organization.

The nearest approach in the Gospels to the Community Rule of Qumran appears in the discourses of Jesus in the First Gospel, especially his directions to the disciples in chapters 10 and 18, with the opening paragraph of chapter 23, where a contrast is drawn between them and the Pharisees. It is possible, indeed, with Krister Stendahl to go farther and recognize in the Gospel of Matthew as a whole a counterpart to the Qumran Community Rule, "a manual for teaching and administration within the church" (*The School of St Matthew*, 1954, p. 35), but in this case we have a manual which includes not only the features of a community rule but guiding lines for Old Testament exegesis also (the counterpart of the Qumran commentaries as well as of the Rule), set in a narrative or kerygmatic framework which has no counterpart in the surviving Qumran literature.

FELLOWSHIP MEAL

To what extent a common meal was a regular and significant feature of Jesus' life with his disciples must be a matter of inference from hints here and there in the Gospels, but we should expect *a priori* that it played some part. The sacramental meaning given to the bread and the cup at the Last Supper ("This is my body . . . this is my covenant blood"), pointing to the death of Jesus as the new passover, is not paralleled at Qumran; but, apart from that, special occasions for the "breaking of the bread" at which Jesus performed the part of head of his "family" in some distinctive fashion (cf. Luke 24. 30f., 35) were apparently continued in the fellowship of his followers when he was no longer visibly with them. In view of the priestly organization of the Qumran community, its fellowship meals may well have reflected the weekly eating of the shewbread by Aaron and his sons (Lev. 24. 5-9), just as its ceremonial washings, exceeding in frequency and importance those of other Jews (even of the purity-conscious Pharisees), may have perpetuated the special washings prescribed for priests. These are features which we should not expect to be imitated in a lay fellowship like that of the disciples of Jesus, who indeed were more lax than most religious Jews in the matter of ceremonial washing (Mark 7. 1ff.). But there is the further possibility that the special meals at Qumran were regarded as anticipating the meal in the age to come, described in the Rule of the Congregation, at which the Messiah would be present (I QSa. ii. 11ff.); in that case we may compare Jesus' statement at the Last Supper that he would not eat the passover again "until it is fulfilled in the kingdom of God" (Luke 22. 15f.; cf. Mark 14. 25; 1 Cor. 11. 26).

The Last Supper, which the Synoptic Evangelists clearly envisage as a passover meal (a view confirmed by the details of the Supper), is equally clearly represented in the Fourth Gospel as being held at least twenty-four hours before the passover meal (a representation supported by some details of the Synoptic narrative). Of all attempts to reconcile the two accounts, the most promising is that of Annie Jaubert in *La date de la Cène* (1957; Eng. tr., 1965); she argues that, while John's record follows the lunisolar calendar which regulated the temple services in Jerusalem, Jesus and his disciples celebrated the passover three days earlier, according to the calendar observed by the Qumran community and some other nonconformist groups among the Jews—the solar calendar previously known to us from the Book of Jubilees. (This book enjoyed high esteem at Qumran, as is plain from CD xvi. 4; Hebrew fragments of it were found in Caves, 1, 2, and 4.)

QUMRAN AND THE FOURTH GOSPEL

Of all the Gospels, it is the Fourth that shows the closest and most numerous affinities with the Qumran literature, to a point where scholars have spoken of a common conceptual reservoir. We shall preserve caution if we recall how practically every fresh discovery in the field of Near Eastern religion from the closing centuries B.C. and the early centuries A.D. has been hailed in its day as the key to the problem of the Fourth Gospel; nevertheless, such characteristic Johannine expressions as "the sons of light", "the light of life", "walking in darkness", "doing the truth", "the works of God" are characteristic also of the Qumran writings—and not the expressions only, but the thought-world which they reflect. In the Qumran and Johannine writings, however, the dualism of this thought-world is not the absolute dualism of its Iranian home; it is a dualism subordinated to the Hebrew belief in one God who created all things good. "From the God of knowledge is everything that is and that is to be; even before they existed, he established all their design": these words from the Qumran Rule (I QS. iii. 15) remind us of the Fourth Evangelist's affirmation about the Logos, "all things were made through him, and without him was not anything made that was made" (John 1. 3).

Yet between the Qumran and Johannine use of this terminology there are differences: above all, in the Fourth Gospel "light", "life" and related concepts are embodied in the incarnate Logos, identified with the historical person Jesus of Nazareth, and they find their interpretation in the events of his ministry.

The early chapters of the Gospel of John record a phase of Jesus' ministry in the south and centre of Palestine concurrent with the closing months of John the Baptist's ministry in those same areas. The dispute about purification mentioned in John 3. 25, which led John's disciples to question Jesus' activity, is the kind of dispute which must have been common when so many competing "baptist" movements were active in those parts. Our reconstruction of the life of the Qumran community provides an illuminating background to these chapters of John. If we try to find a personal link between the community (or the general movement to which it belonged) and the Fourth Gospel, we may (bearing in mind what is said elsewhere in this volume about John the Baptist) reflect on the high probability that the Beloved Disciple, whose testimony underlies this Gospel, was a disciple of John the Baptist before he began to follow Jesus (cf. John 1. 35-40 with 21. 24). Not that the affinities which have been mentioned are to be explained in terms of one individual link; we must think also of "the life of an on-going community" (J. A. T. Robinson, *Twelve New Testament Studies*, 1962, p. 106).

JESUS AND THE TEACHER OF RIGHTEOUSNESS

As the Qumran community owes its character and outlook pre-eminently to the personality and teaching of the Teacher of Righteousness, so primitive Christianity owes its being to Jesus.

A comparison of Jesus and the Teacher of Righteousness is difficult because of the allusiveness of the Qumran references to the Teacher and the uncertainty of any reconstruction of his career; even the most sceptical assessment of the historical element in the Gospels among contemporary New Testament students leaves us with much more definite information about the historical Jesus than the Qumran documents provide about the Teacher. One thing must be said: in any such comparison apologetic motives have no place. It is foolish to imagine that the significance of Jesus can be enhanced by depreciation of one of the righteous men who went before him. Yet the words "who went before him" are appropriate in more than a chronological sense. The formulation of Jesus' indictment which was fastened to his cross, "The King of the Jews", indicates that he was held to have made some sort of messianic claim for himself, and he was certainly proclaimed by his followers very soon after-wards as the Messiah of Israel. There is no indication that any messianic claim was made for the Teacher of Righteousness either by himself or by his followers: his role was rather that of a fore-runner of the messianic age, "to make ready for the Lord a people prepared" (cf. Luke 1. 17). Of the manner of his death we have no information, nor yet about any significance that was attached to it, save that with it a final probationary period of forty years was believed to begin (CD xx. 14 f.; cf. the implied interpretation of the forty years of Ps. 95. 10 in Heb. 3. 7ff.). It is quite uncertain whether his resurrection is implied in the reference to the "standing up of one who will teach righteousness in the end of days" (CD vi. 10 f.); it is, indeed, quite uncertain whether the Qumran community held the doctrine of resurrection or not. But it is nowhere suggested that, if such an expectation was entertained with regard to the Teacher, he ever did rise again or that anyone thought he did so. Apart from his qualities as an organizer and leader of men, his main service to his followers appears to have been his creative biblical exegesis. Jesus too taught his followers the principles of a creative biblical exegesis, and while they might not have regarded this as his main service to them, it provided them with the frame-work for understanding and declaring the meaning of his person and work.

Another essay in this collection deals with the messianic doctrine of the Qumran community. Here it may suffice to say that the messianic doctrine of Qumran, especially as it related to the Messiah of Israel and his career of conquest, was repudiated by Jesus as decisively as other current forms of messianic expectation. If anal-ogies are sought in Old Testament prophecy for Jesus' understand-ing and fulfilment of his mission, they may be found more readily in a combination of the Servant of Yahweh of Isa. 42—53 and the "one like a son of man" of Dan. 7. 13 than in the explicit messianic passages.

While the Servant of Yahweh and the Son of Man do not figure expressly in the Qumran literature, the influence of the biblical passages where they are portrayed can be discerned in the thought and language of the community. The speaker in some of the Hymns of Thanksgiving—whether he is the Teacher of Righteousness in person or an anonymous spokesman of the community—describes his experiences in terms of the obedient and suffering Servant. More important still: the community as a whole seems to have regarded itself as called upon corporately to fulfil the Servant's role. As the Teacher and his followers devoted themselves to the study and practice of the law of God, as they endured persecution and privation for righteousness' sake, they believed that they were accumulating a store of merit which would be accepted as an atonement for the polluted land of Israel. But they also believed that, when the "epoch of wickedness" came to an end, it would be their privilege to be God's instruments in the execution of judgement against the ungodly (cf. I QpHab. v. 3-6). These two phases of corporate fulfilment of prophecy may be compared with Jesus' words about the Son of Man, on the one hand suffering rejection and giving his life a ransom for many, on the other hand coming in glory to acknowledge faithful confessors and to disown the faithless in the presence of God and the holy angels. The corporate aspect is not absent from the Gospels: Jesus speaks of his followers as both sharing his cup of passion and sharing his throne of glory with him.

COMMON BACKGROUND

Here we have probably the most telling affinities between Qumran and the Gospels. They imply on the one hand the distinctive and divergent emphases of the Teacher of Righteousness and the Prophet of Nazareth; they imply on the other hand a common background more particularly defined than the general background of Hebrew scripture and Israel's history. This more particular common background has been recognized—outstandingly by Matthew Black in *The Scrolls and Christian Origins* (1961)—in a nonconformist tradition going quite a long way back in Israel's story, and one which towards the end of the pre-Christian era gained rather than lost in strength, existing both in a northern and in a southern group. The Psalms of Solomon (mid-first century B.C.) and the first two chapters of Luke (with their messianic canticles) reflect the piety and hope of the southern group. Further study of this nonconformist tradition, with the wealth of new evidence provided by the Dead Sea Scrolls, is likely to throw additional welcome light on the Qumran community and on its relation to Jesus and the Gospels.

7

DUALISM, GNOSTICISM, AND OTHER ELEMENTS IN THE PRE-PAULINE TRADITION

MAX WILCOX

THE texts from Qumran at first sight appear thoroughly Jewish, even if perhaps not reflecting the more "orthodox" stream in Judaism. They are steeped in the Old Testament, and in certain ways display an attitude to the Law rather stricter than that of the Pharisees.[1] There is, then, some reason for seeing them as standing even further away from the outlook of Jesus than the Rabbinic writings do. On the other hand, there are elements in them which recall very strikingly patterns of thought found in a variety of places in the New Testament, especially the Fourth Gospel, the Pauline letters, the Letter to the Hebrews, and the Book of Revelation. There is therefore some justification for suspecting that behind this group of writings there may have been some more tangible factor at work.

In this paper then we shall turn our attention to an examination of a number of elements in the Scrolls which appear to have affinities with ideas found in the New Testament and which—to be precise—seem to anticipate to some extent certain of the otherwise distinctive features of the thought of Paul.

I

One such characteristic of the Scrolls is their apparently dualistic world-view. It is reflected in much of their terminology, and finds its clearest and most unambiguous form in the passage from the Manual of Discipline setting out the so-called "doctrine of the Two Spirits" (I QS. iii. 13—iv. 26). We may mention here the use of expressions such as "Sons of Light", "Sons of Darkness", "the men

of God's lot" (I QS. ii. 2; I QM. i. 5, etc.), "the men of Belial's lot"
(I QS. ii. 5, I QM. i. 5, etc.) "the Spirit of Truth", "the Spirit of Error"'
and so on. One is instantly reminded of passages from the New
Testament such as 2 Cor. 6. 14—7. 1, 1 John 4. 6, and others. Let us
then turn to I QS. iii. 13—iv. 26, and examine what it says.

This passage looks like a kind of "creed" or block of special
teaching. In a way it seems to interrupt the sequence and introduce
something unexpected into its context. Further, it opens with the
phrase *le maskil*, which might mean "for instruction", "to instruct",
or simply, "for the instructor/teacher". The term *maskil* also occurs
in the Old Testament, in the titles to some of the Psalms,[2] and in
Daniel.[3] The use and construction here is very similar in many ways
to that found in I QSb. i. 1—the "Collection of Blessings"—"Words
of Blessing. For the *Maskil*, to bless those who [fear God and do] his
will . . ." It introduces or heads the preamble to the list of
"blessings", which then properly begins in I QSb. i. 3b. Again, in
I QSb. iii. 2ob, we find the list closed with an explanatory statement,
which is then followed in line 22 by a repetition of the words just
mentioned previously, viz., "Words of blessing. For the *Maskil*, to
bless the sons of Zadok, the priests, . . .". Yet another series begins
similarly in I QSb. v. 20, and this time it is even closer in form to the
passage we began by considering: "For the *Maskil*, to bless the Prince
of the Community. . . ." From a consideration of these cases and
also others from CD xii. 21, xiii. 22 and I QS. ix. 12, 21, we seem
entitled to regard the term as a name for a particular officer of the
group, whose duty is the instruction of the community in special
teaching.[4] Certain other passages where the verb is used suggest
that this teaching is possibly secret; certainly it is used of instructing
the "perfect of way", and is employed in parallel with "giving the
upright understanding in the knowledge of the Most High and the
wisdom of the Sons of Heaven", in the very passage from I QS with
which we began.[5] More of this later, when we look at the possibility
of Gnostic elements or influences. Meantime we shall content ourselves with observing that the present passages, I QS. iii. 13—iv. 26,
would appear to be special teaching, and may even merit the
description "secret".

It tells us that "all that is and shall be comes from the God of
Knowledge" (iii. 15). Before such things came into existence, he
laid out their plan, so that when they do come into being, they carry
it out to the letter—"according to his glorious purpose"—and there
is no changing it (iii. 15-16; cf. James 1. 17-18). He created man "to
rule the world" (iii. 17-18; cf. Gen. 1. 26ff.), and appointed for him
two spirits by which to frame his conduct "until the appointed time
of his visitation". These are "the Spirit of Truth" and "the Spirit of

Error". Thus, during the period intervening between the creation of man and God's day of "visitation", man has these two spirits striving within his heart [better, "mind"] for control of him (iv. 23). The Spirit of Error [or the Angel of Darkness or Belial, as he is called] and his fellows try to "trip" the Sons of Light (iii. 24; cf. Mark 13. 22). Perhaps this might happen, were it not that the God of Israel and his Angel of Truth (the Spirit of Truth, the Prince of Lights) helped them. God had appointed the two spirits "in equal shares" until the Endtime, or what I QS terms "the renewal" (iv. 25; cf. 2 Cor. 5. 17, Rev. 21. 5; Isa. 43. 19, 65. 17, 66. 22, etc.). When this takes place, wrongdoing will be destroyed forever, "the truth of the world" (eternal truth?) will appear, and to those whom God has chosen he will grant understanding of the "knowledge of the Most High, the wisdom of the sons of Heaven [God?]";[6] theirs will be "all the glory of Adam [or, 'man']" (I QS. iv. 22-23). That is, they would presumably be permitted to have that glory which was originally and rightfully Adam's, but which he forfeited at the Fall. In the present time however—"all the days of Belial's rule" (i. 18, 24; ii. 19; etc),—evil is allowed a limited existence (cf. Rev. 22. 10-11), and mankind is thus divided into two mutually hostile camps, "the sons of darkness" and "the sons of light".

This apparent dualism of the "two spirits" does not seem at first sight to be derived from the Old Testament. On the other hand, it does occur to some extent in Jubilees, Enoch, and Testaments of the XII Patriarchs,[7] and also, seemingly, in 1 John 4. 6. Looking a little further, the dualism between "light" and "darkness", the "Prince of Lights" [or God?] and "Belial", appears to have a parallel in 2 Cor. 6. 14—7. 1, a notoriously difficult section which interrupts its context and has often been thought to have been originally independent of it. Now 2 Cor. 6. 15 is the sole place in the New Testament where "Belial" is mentioned, let alone contrasted directly with Christ. However it is highly improbable that I QS was influenced by 2 Cor. 6 14ff., although there may have been some connection between the two, or both may reflect a common basic tradition. Be that as it may, we have an apparently dualistic scheme in I QS and certain related texts, together with indications of a similar pattern in certain New Testament passages. What is the origin of it, if it is not traceable to the Old Testament?

From an early date a ready answer to this question has been found by not a few scholars in the possibility of Iranian influence.[8] Indeed, this has long been discussed in connection with Jewish apocalyptic in general, and the claim was made in the case of the so-called Zadokite documents (CD) soon after their discovery in 1896–7. Moreover, the possibility of some kind of connection with

6

the rise of Gnosticism has also been raised. What are we to say about all this?

We must begin by observing that in the Iranian sources we do indeed meet with several basic traits which seem present in the Scrolls. (*a*) the existence of one wise lord, God, "Ahura Mazda"; (*b*) the co-existence from all eternity of [his] two or "twin" spirits, the Holy Spirit (Spenta Mainyu) and the Evil Spirit (Angra Mainyu), responsibile for the good and evil creations respectively; these two are fundamentally and ceaselessly (?) opposed; (*c*) an apocalypticism which looks to an end of the evil order : the "abode of light" for all the followers of "truth", "darkness" for all the followers of the "lie". However, at what seems to be a yet later stage in the tradition, Ahura Mazda appears to have been identified with the Good or Holy Spirit, Spenta Mainyu, so that Angra Mainyu now becomes his eternal opponent. Here we have a true dualism not really represented in the earlier material. This is of some importance, for if we press the claim for Iranian influence, it must be to the "earlier" stratum that we look. It is no good trying to see in Belial an *equal and eternal* opponent or counterpart to God : he is created, dependent; just another piece of God's creation, and so has no ultimately independent existence of his own, let alone creative power.

On the other hand, it has been pointed out that there are also certain features of I QS. iii. 13—iv. 26 which suggest affinities with later stages of Iranian religion, e.g., the roles played by "light" and darkness". Thus, if some relationship does in fact exist—and it can certainly not be excluded in advance—it would seem to be rather more complicated than a simple case of direct dependence. Next, the Iranian texts—like those at Qumran—show us mankind divided into two camps: just as the two primeval spirits had once *chosen* to follow good and evil respectively,[9] so also mankind had made a similar choice. That decision determines their destiny, for like the Qumran teaching again, an end is seen for the activity of the followers of the "lie". In I QS. iii. 13—iv. 26, however, it is not the decision of the two spirits nor that of mankind which determines our fate, but God's own choice, made prior to the existence of all things. This point, as we have already seen, is most unequivocally made in I QS. iii. 15-16. Professor Karl G. Kuhn, who was a pioneer in the matter of possible Iranian influence in the Scrolls, sees this point of difference as connected with the Jewish monotheistic idea of God developed from the Old Testament, i.e., the idea of creation.[10]

There are however further difficulties in the way of this theory. First, there is the absence of precise information regarding the age, actual content, and development of ancient Persian religion (in the pre-Sassanidian period). Next, there is the fact that the men of Qumran—whatever else they may have been or believed—regarded themselves as Jews, and very strict ones at that: far more "exclusive" than the Pharisees. If they were influenced by Persian ideas, it seems inherently improbable that such influence was at all conscious. If indeed such parallels as there are really relate to the older stratum of Iranian religion then we may—even on this hypothesis—have to look back possibly as far as the Exile or Persian period for the links. Again, parallels of language, and even of underlying thought-forms and "mythology" do not necessarily prove more than the literature we are considering was a child of its age. The essential point here is that the "dualism" of Qumran is not a true one. It thus may have features in common with the older Iranian views described above, but there is then also no real reason why it should be seen as wholly foreign to the Old Testament. We should be justified in regarding it as an attempt to present what its writers firmly believed to be genuine Old Testament teaching in thought-forms more appropriate to its own day and circumstances. This is all the more to the point in view of the fact that the Old Testament in certain places at least is not without signs of Persian influence.

On the other hand an attempt to see in the passage under discussion parallels with Gnostic thought is no more helpful. The dualism of Qumran is clearly an "ethical" one: the "marks" of the "Spirit of Truth" and the "Spirit of Error" are set out clearly enough in I QS. iv. 2-6 and 9-11 respectively, passages which remind us of the lists of virtues and vices appearing in certain places in the New Testament, especially Gal. 5. 18-23. The human race, although divided temporarily into two opposed groups, owes its creation to the one God: likewise the two spirits, the good along with the evil. In this way it is not only strikingly unlike the metaphysical dualism of Gnosticism, but also strongly reminiscent of the Rabbinical teaching on the "two impulses"—the Good Impulse (*yetser hatob*) and the Evil Impulse (*yetser hara'*). Both of these were the work of the one God, and although one passage tells us that at the End, in the "world to come" God will destroy the Evil Impulse in the presence of the righteous and the wicked,[11] yet it is nevertheless God's creation every bit as much as the Good Impulse, and there is no sense in which it may be thought of as independent of and opposed to him. Further, the presence of the terms "light" and "darkness" in the language of Qumran does not in itself indicate an affinity to Gnostic thought. The "sons of light" and the "sons of darkness" alike live in the same world: the "sons of light" are not viewed as if part of another, and "higher", order of being. Moreover, in spite of what has been written on the subject, decisive evidence for a belief in either resurrection or immortality is simply not available so far. The few passages which some scholars take as referring to an after-life do not bear the weight put upon them. This fact in itself does not prove that the sect did not hold such a belief, but it can scarcely help us in finding parallels with Gnosticism. This matter we shall turn to next, but here it may be sufficient for us to say that the material before us does not warrant the inference of (direct) Iranian influence, nor—at least in regard to the "dualism"— does it indicate the presence of "gnostic" ideas. But this question must be considered in its own right.

2

When we speak of "gnosticism", we must be very careful in our use of terms, for if we hope to find in the Scrolls a highly developed system of thought like those, e.g., of Marcion or Basilides, we shall certainly only do so by performing a great deal of fanciful exegesis. The proper question is rather whether, and if so, to what extent, the basic elements of "gnostic" thought can be detected in the Scrolls. Reduced to bare essentials, this movement involved the view that the world was inherently evil. Within this world the "divine spark" had become imprisoned in certain men, for whom alone "salvation" was possible. That salvation took place only when the devotee, in whom the "divine spark" is imprisoned, attained "knowledge" (*gnōsis*) of God, that is, of himself, where he had come from (the Divine fire, Great First Light, etc.), and where he was going (back to God). When the "soul" knows itself, it is thus "deified". So it is that this "knowledge" of God/self is also knowledge of the "way" to God. But such knowledge is not for everyone; it is only for the "few"—those in whom the "divine spark" has been imprisoned. He who has it (*gnōsis*) is saved already; he who has not, is lost. Nevertheless *gnōsis* is itself a gift from God. Thus in many forms of gnostic speculation it is conveyed by a "Redeemer" who, like the "divine spark", comes down from the heavenly realms to impart *gnōsis* to his own.

If we turn now to the Scrolls, we do in fact find the presence of a good number of words and phrases which at first sight might suggest some kind of relationship with Gnosticism. We have already referred earlier to the "dualism" of the Scrolls; but in addition there is the frequent use of words for "knowledge", "insight", "under-standing", "perfection" (especially, "perfection of way"), along with various words for "secret" and "mystery". Do the Scrolls have Gnostic elements after all?

It is convenient to begin with the words related to the idea of "knowledge". Let us state at the outset that although the words *da'at, de'ah,* (knowledge) occur fairly frequently in the Scrolls, they certainly do not have a uniform meaning: the actual significance varies considerably from context to context. It may refer to man's knowledge, but in our documents when it does it seems to mean some special aspect of that knowledge. For example, in I QS. iii. 1 and I QH. xi. 8, it is used in phrases whose parallel member includes the word for "righteousness" or "justice". Likewise in I QS. viii. 9, ix. 17. In these cases it probably means knowledge of the Torah. Sometimes its context indicates a relationship to God's mighty deeds (I QH. xi. 28), while in a number of other passages it seems that some kind of Divine revelation is involved (see especially I QS. iv. 22, ix. 19, xi. 3, 6, I QH. iv. 18). A quite different slant is given in a group of cases where the knowledge is not man's knowledge of God, but rather God's own knowledge. We may briefly list here I QS. iii. 15, I QH. i. 26, xii 10, and f. 8, 9, ("the God of Knowledge"), cf. 1 Sam. 2. 3; I QS. iv. 22 (cf. Num. 24. 16, the Balaam oracle—though here it is not quite clear whether the knowledge is God's, or of God, in the Scroll text); finally, I QS. xi. 3, 11, 18, where the thought is of God's own knowledge, in the two last cases of his "knowledge" as having a role in the creation of all things (or of "the ALL"?).

Before we go on to discuss the last pair, which in many ways seem among the most interesting, we should observe that in several cases at least, terms and phrases containing the word "knowledge" appear to have been taken from passages of the Old Testament. Moreover, in one case we know that the Old Testament section in question was a favourite portion with the authors of the Scrolls (viz., Num. 24. 16ff).[12] This is also true of the expression "spirit of knowledge" (I QS. iv. 4, I QSb. v. 25, and I QH. xiv. 25), apparently related to Isa. 11. 2. We shall return to this point in a moment. But for the present it is interesting to raise the question whether the authors of the scrolls sought out such phrases in the Old Testament to support their case, or whether it was not rather their familiarity with such (messianic?) passages which prompted the uses in question.

The similarity of I QS. xi. 11 (and also 18) to John 1. 3 has rightly been described as "striking".[13] The passage runs:

> By his knowledge all things ["all"?] came into being.
> And all things ["all"?] existed—
> By his purpose [s] did he order it,
> And apart from him was nothing made.

With it we should consider also xi. 17-18 :

> Thou hast taught all knowledge,
> And all that exists exists by thy good pleasure,
> And beside thee there is no other. . . .

These passages certainly do recall John 1. 3, and perhaps we should add Col. 1. 15-17. But is it really necessary to seek here some "gnostic" influence? Would not an appeal to the Old Testament suffice? Before we attempt an answer, let us look at another verse from the same section of I QS, viz. xi. 6ff.

> . . . My eye has gazed upon understanding,
> Which was concealed from men of knowledge,
> and [upon] wise counsel [hidden]from the sons of men."

Reicke's comment that in this passage God's knowledge is identified with his providence as in Rom. 11. 33, seems astray.[14] Reference to Rom. 11. 33, even if appropriate, would not help Reicke's case, for— apart from the Old Testament quotations in vv. 34-35,[15]—it looks very like a piece of pre-Pauline material, and has a distinctively "gnostic" tone to it. At all events verse 33 contains no less than three favourite Gnostic terms in half a verse.[16] But perhaps the puzzling logion of Matt. 11. 25-30, Luke 10. 21-22, and 1 Cor. 2. 6-16 present even closer parallels. These too are quite notable for their apparent affinity to, or at least awareness of, some aspects of gnostic thought. Nevertheless, although the language used in these passages has a gnostic ring to it, the actual material itself is not in conflict with the basic beliefs and outlook of Judaism and Christianity. What does seem to be indicated is a borrowing of gnostic terminology, or at least a coming to grips with it.

Let us return now to the examples mentioned above, where the use of the term "knowledge" appeared in some way related to that found in a specific Old Testament passage, especially in some text known to have been used by the Qumran writers elsewhere in their scrolls. The cases noted are not the only ones. In I QS. i. 11-12, iii. 2, the word "knowledge" forms part of an expository addition or gloss on the *Shema* interpreting "heart", and seems to portray one way in which God is to be "loved". I QS. ii. 3 gives a similar treatment of the Aaronic Blessing, ". . . may he be gracious unto thee *with eternal knowledge* . . .". Comparison of the Qumran elaborations of the Aaronic Blessing (I QS. ii. 1b-4a, cf. ii. 4b-10, etc.) with those of later Rabbinic Judaism reveals fascinating parallels. M. Weise, in a monograph on the subject, finds correspondence "in every case in sense, in some instances even to the letter".[17] This he rightly traces not to mutual dependence nor to use of a common source, but to "a common Jewish exegetical tradition . . . shared by our group and Rabbinic Judaism alike . . .".[18] Such a tradition should however be dated to a period even earlier than our documents, and this in itself is an important point. On the phrase "eternal knowledge" itself, the context—including the parallel use of the term "knowledge of life" in the previous line—indicates that it refers to some thing that is a gift from God. The Rabbinical parallels produced by Weise regard that knowledge as "knowledge of Torah".[19] This however would suit the outlook of the Scrolls admirably. For example, I QS. v. 2 refers to those who "separate themselves from the council of the men of Error, to become a Fellowship in *Torah and property* . . .". In the comments added to the *Shema*, the words are "with all knowledge and strength and wealth". From these and other cases we may draw a parallel between "Torah" on the one hand and "knowledge and strength" on the other. Or again, I QS. i. 12 gives one of the main aims of the Community as being "to illumine their knowledge by the truth of God's ordinances . . .". Knowledge, then, in these places, is closely related to "knowledge of Torah", and many other passages indicate clearly the centrality of study of Torah in the life of the sect. Thus also, the word *sekhel* "understanding", a partial synonym of "knowledge" is found used in several places parallel to the phrase "(his) deeds in Torah".

What of the other apparently gnostic ideas we mentioned earlier in this section, viz., "perfection", "secret(s)", "mysteries", etc.? Once again, the motif of "Torah" appears. Thus, the term *tamim*. "perfect" occurs quite frequently in the Scrolls. Again and again the reference is to "perfection of way", i.e., to conduct; for instance, in I QS. i. 13, xi. 2, etc. The very Community itself is to be ". . . a most holy abode for Aaron, . . . a house of perfection and truth in Israel . . .". The whole life of the sect is aimed at fulfilment of Torah: positively, by study of it, meditation upon it, and "deeds in Torah"; negatively, by abstention from all that confers uncleanness and impurity, or might involve the slightest departure from Torah. This great emphasis on meticulous keeping of Torah and on "purity" is required by the view that the community constituted in some sense the true Temple, and that "holy angels" were present in its midst. The members are "faithful witnesses" in a perverse generation, they are also conceived of as participating in God's final Holy War against the "sons of darkness" and the "Kittim". As such, "purity" must be their watchword, for the angels are also present in their battle-camp (I QM. vii. 6; cf. Deut. 23. 14 (Heb. 15)). Other texts suggest that the sect somehow participates in the heavenly liturgy, while several MSS deal with the New Jerusalem, the New Temple, and its cult.

There remains the group of words meaning "secret", "mystery", along with passages where secrecy is enjoined. How far was the group esoteric? W. D. Davies, discussing "knowledge", noted several cases where that knowledge seems to be secret, either expressly, or by implication, viz., I QS. ix. 17, 22; viii. 18, and possibly x. 25, v. 11f.[20] The first two of these are fairly clear, and in both "conceal-ment" and "secrecy" are enjoined. Likewise, I QS. viii. 18 directs that knowledge of the counsel of the "holy men" is withheld from the new member, until his deeds are "pure": it is only for the inner circle. The other cases he adduces seem rather less convincing. Then there are the words *raz* and *sod* (secret), and *nistar* (hidden), which occur rather often. Do these suggest gnostic influence or content? Perhaps we should observe at the outset that Gnostics were not the only people who strove to keep things to themselves. Again, the fact that *raz* is a word of Persian origin contributes nothing, in view of its frequent occurrence in Daniel, where we also find forms based on the root *str*. Indeed, rather than look for extraneous influences, we would do better to appreciate the links between the thought of Daniel (and other Jewish apocalyptic texts) and that of the Scrolls. Further, in Psalm 19. 12, the word *nistarot* occurs, meaning "hidden things": the actual words are "knowledge of hidden things" (cf. I QS. v. 11). Now this passage is mentioned in the Damascus Document (CD iii. 14ff.) as referring to "errors in the observance of sabbaths and other holy seasons". The "knowledge" here enables the sect to keep the Torah correctly in regard to the calendar. Again, the words, "revealing his secrets to this servants the prophets" (cf. Amos 3. 7), appear in various forms. In such cases the "secret knowledge" seems to relate to knowing the secrets of the End-time, (cf. e.g., I QS. xi. 3, I QpHab. ii. 9, vii. 5). This view is supported by reference to a host of other passages where verses from the Old Testament (especially from the Prophets) are reinterpreted as applying to events either eschatological in nature, or historical but seen as eschatological.

Was the sect at Qumran a Gnostic one? If we restrict the meaning of "gnostic" to "having to do with secret knowledge of the mind and will of God", perhaps we may be led to answer yes. But if we are looking for a way of salvation expressed in terms of some kind of knowledge apart from Torah and "deeds in Torah", or for the presence and activity of a redeemer-revealer figure, historical or mythological, or indeed an emphasis on knowledge in its own right, we shall have to say no. The much discussed "Teacher of Righteous-ness", whether he really existed or was only an eschatological fiction, is certainly not a "redeemer": he is one who teaches or taught correct understanding of Torah, and gives or gave instruction

concerning what God would do to the last generation (cf. CD i.
11-12, vi. 10-11, xx. 27bff., I QpHab. v. 10-12, vii. 4, viii. 1-3, etc.).
The fact that he seems (if he was in fact historical) to have suffered
persecution, does not suit the role of a gnostic redeemer-figure
(I QpHab. xi. 4-8). His mission was not one of "salvation" except in
the sense that he sought to stir his group to the most thorough and
thorough-going obedience to Torah, for this alone was the way to
God. Even the astral and calendaric texts from Qumran seem
basically aimed at ensuring that God's law is kept to the very letter,
in this case in the matter of correct timing of sabbaths, festivals,
and hours of prayer. In all these ways the Scrolls stand very much
nearer to Pharisaism than to Gnosticism (or indeed, Christianity),
revealing in fact an even stricter and more unbending attitude to the
Torah and the keeping of it.

3

This brings us to our final problem. Paul's attitude to the Torah is
clearly in striking contrast with that of the Scrolls—an outlook he
shares with Jesus. Nevertheless, there are ideas and passages in his
letters which seem to recall the beliefs and sometimes the words of
certain sections of the writings from Qumran. What are we to say
about this? The further fact that these elements in Paul do not
appear confined to his writings, but appear in other parts of the
New Testament, has been taken as suggesting that some kind of
common source of influence is to be suspected. How then are we
to evaluate the question of the origin of these "pre-Pauline" ideas?
Let us consider some of them in turn.

(a) *The Community as God's Temple.* In several places in Paul's
writings, and other books at least very closely related to his works,
there are references to Christians as constituting "the temple of
God", e.g., 2 Cor. 6. 16, 1 Cor. 3. 16-17, Eph. 2. 20-22, and 1 Cor. 6.
19 (where the expression "temple of the Holy Spirit" is applied to
the actual body of the believer). In a valuable study of the more
general question of the Temple motif in Qumran and the New
Testament, Bertil Gärtner deals with the first three of the passages
listed, along with 1 Tim. 3. 15, and draws attention to the similarity
of thought to that found in various texts from Qumran, for instance,
I QS. viii. 7ff, ix. 2ff, and especially IV Q Flor. i. 3ff, 14ff, 16ff, etc.[21]
We should probably add here the references in Col. 1. 12 (cf. Eph. 1.
11-18, Acts 20. 32, 26. 18), to the Christians participating in the
portion of the lot of the "saints" in light. These passages—with
which we should also compare I QS. xi. 7-8, I QH. xi. 11-12,—
may reflect Wisd. 5. 5; but there are also grounds for suspecting

that the element in question was "a piece of independently circulating traditional material".[22] Further support may be cited from I QSb. iv. 25, and IV QSl. 39 and 40, where the closest relationship is seen between the heavenly and the earthly liturgies. Now this "temple" motif is not confined to the Pauline writings. It is therefore likely that it was not a genuine Pauline idea, but indeed entered the thought of Paul—and also that of other New Testament writers— from "outside". The question is, whether we are justified in looking to Qumran for the origin of it. In this connection Gärtner notes that while the Epistles reflect a collective view of the temple, akin to that of Qumran, the Gospels stress its replacement by "an individual", namely Jesus. To some extent a reconciliation between these two viewpoints might be sought in the theme of Jesus as the "foundation" (1 Cor. 3. 11, Eph. 2. 20ff.) with which is related the "rock/ stone" motif (Rom. 9. 33, applied to Jesus in Rom. 10. 11; cf. 1 Peter 2. 4ff, esp. v. 6): it is worth noting that Isa. 28. 16, which underlies the passages just mentioned, is reflected in I QH. vi. 25ff, I QS. viii. 4ff, and perhaps in IV QpIsa^d. 1-3 (based on Isa. 54. 11), although the latter may refer not so much to "temple" thinking as to "Jerusalem"-motifs (cf. Gal. 4. 27). It would nevertheless be very risky indeed to argue here for mutual dependence. A common stream of interpretation is the most the facts require.

(*b*) *Discipline.*   There is one tricky passage in 1 Cor. 5. 1ff which study of the Scrolls may help illuminate. It deals with the disciplinary act of "handing over N.N. to Satan for destruction of the flesh . . .". M. Weise has pointed out an interesting parallel in CD xix. 13ff, where all who enter the Covenant but do not keep its decrees are to be visited with destruction at the hand of Belial. Elsewhere the "destroying angels" have this duty (e.g., CD ii. 5ff, I QS. iv. 11-13). The act of "handing over" the offender for destruction is a judicial act of the Community, according to I QS. viii. 6b-7a, and is related to the curse in I QS. ii. 10. Weise cites further New Testament parallels in Acts 5. 1ff, 8. 18ff, and Matt. 5. 22.[23]

(*c*) *Flesh and Spirit.*   Paul and John alike make use of the contrast, "flesh-spirit", and it may be asked whether it is not in fact independent of both. But if so, it does not appear due to either the Old Testament or to the thought of Rabbinic Judaism as we know it, without further qualification. And in Gnostic thought, the spirit sought to escape from the flesh, not to oppose it as such. In the Scrolls however the word "flesh" seems to have two meanings: on the whole, it represents "humanity" and is a quite neutral term; occasionally, though, it seems to have a moral overtone, and is used in close conjunction with words like "sin", "iniquity", etc. (One of the better examples of this is I QS. xi. 12: ". . . in the iniquity of the flesh"). K. G. Kuhn has argued that these two types of meaning for "flesh" correspond to those we find in the Paulines, and quotes instances like Rom. 7. 14, 17-20, 25, Gal. 5. 17, etc. Further, in the Scrolls the spirit of the pious, i.e., "the spirit of truth", puts a man "in the battlefront on God's side against the Evil One". We thus meet the "dualism" of "flesh-spirit" with which we began. In this connection the presence in the Qumran texts of the expression "the body of flesh" (I QpHab. ix. 2, IV QpNah. ii. 6) strikingly recalls the similar phrase in Col. 1. 22, 2. 11 (but cf. also Ecclus. 23. 16, Enoch 16. 1). He thus sees it as a "technical term" in Judaism.[24] The presence of many other elements familiar from the Scrolls, in Colossians (and also indeed in Ephesians), strengthens the possibility that we may have some sign here of influence, or at least contact between the two groups of writings. (Of these, we may refer in passing to Col. 2. 16, on food, drink, sabbaths, etc., likewise Col. 2. 20ff on asceticism, the remarks about special knowledge, and angel-worship, Col. 2. 18, among others.) W. D. Davies, on the other hand, has pointed out that in the Qumran documents the true dualism is not between "flesh" and "spirit" but rather between the "spirit of truth" and "the spirit of error": thus "Paul shares its [the sect's] terminology at certain points but not its doctrinal formulations".[25] A serious difficulty is the fact that Paul cannot be said to refer to "the spirit of error" as such at all: the only cases where it can be argued that he does are far from certain (1 Cor. 2. 12, Eph. 2. 2). The outcome would seem to be that although there are strong hints of the use of some common terminology, direct influence is not proven.

(*d*) *Other elements.* Among other matters we may mention the use of the term "Sons of light" (of Christians) in 1 Thess. 5. 5, the odd phrase about angels in 1 Cor. 11. 10 (perhaps recalling the Qumran thought of the presence of angels at meetings of the Community, see above), the striking section, 2 Cor. 6. 14—7. 1, with its numerous echoes of language and thought similar to that of Qumran (e.g., separation, darkness and light, "Belial", etc.). Yet another is the thought of "new creation" (cf. 2 Cor. 5. 17; I QS. iv. 25, where its eschatological sense is quite clear). Others, such as "justification", seem rather less certain. The sect did interpret Hab. 2. 4 in terms of the faith of the "doers of the Law" in the Teacher of Righteousness (I QpHab. viii. 1-3), and in some places ascribes "righteousness" or "justification" of the believer to God and his gift (I QS. xi. 11ff). But how far we can build a case on this for a relationship with the thought of Paul is quite another matter. The legalism of Qumran remains a very weighty obstacle in the way of such an identification.

Where do we go from here? How are we in fact to evaluate the material we have been considering? In the first place we have seen that there is in certain places at least quite strong evidence for some kind of contact between Qumran (or its thought-world) and emergent Christianity. This is, of course, hardly surprising, but as a result many things previously obscure, or thought to be due to the influence of non-Jewish factors, are seen in a new light. Part of this is due to the fact that we no longer need to see first century Judaism solely through the eyes of the New Testament, the Mishnah, and writers like Josephus: we have first-hand sources for movements which—however they may have been regarded in the first century A.D., or at least, prior to the Fall of Jerusalem in A.D. 70,— would have been treated as distinctly heretical or non-orthodox thereafter. Yet it was in this less "case-hardened" period that Christianity emerged. Next, we must note that the contacts with Qumran thought—real or apparent—are much closer in those parts of Paul's writing (and John's too, for that matter) where he is attempting to *counter* something: Colossians, Ephesians (if by Paul), Galatians too, and of course, 2 Cor. 6. 14—7. 1, etc., come to mind. Contact is one thing, dependence is quite another. Finally, and on the same theme, we must never forget the great differences in outlook between the Pauline open-ended Gospel, and the close, exclusiveness of Qumran.

8

THE DEAD SEA SCROLLS AND CHRISTIAN ORIGINS

MATTHEW BLACK

How are we to evaluate the Dead Sea Scrolls for the study of Christian origins? In the Preface to my book, *The Scrolls and Christian Origins*, (Edinburgh, 1961), I quoted the judgement of the well-known American orientalist and distinguished contributor to this collection of essays, W. F. Albright, who wrote, in 1951: "The new evidence with regard to the beliefs and practices of Jewish sectarians of the last two centuries B.C. bids fair to revolutionize our approach to the beginnings of Christianity."[1] In the same vein M. Dupont-Sommer of the Sorbonne, a pioneer in the subject, declared: "All the problems relative to primitive Christianity henceforth find themselves placed in a new light, which forces us to reconsider them completely."[2] Both these opinions were given in the first flush of enthusiasm for the new discoveries, and subsequent studies have led to more temperate statements; but the view is nevertheless hardening among scholars that it is from this side of Judaism that Christianity took its origins. Now, some twenty years later, Professor F. M. Cross of Harvard writes: "The documents from the Wilderness of Judah throw a brilliant light upon the creative and fluid period before the crystallization of Jewish and Christian orthodoxy, and clarify thereby a crucial moment in the emergence of western civilization."[3]

This creative and fluid period in Judaism is one which can only be adequately characterized as that of a widespread and vigorous Jewish sectarianism, a kind of Jewish non-conformity,[4] opposed to the official (predominantly Pharisaic) Judaism of Jerusalem, centred on the Temple and the Jerusalem Sanhedrin. It was represented in the North by strongly anti-Jerusalem, anti-Pharisaic Samaritan groups (Galilee fell well within the sphere of influence of these powerful Samaritan sectaries). In the South its best known representative was the monastic or semi-monastic sect of the Essenes, located by the ancient historians at the Dead Sea, and quite certainly to be identified with the sect of the scrolls. These were fissiparous groups, but they were solidly united in their opposition to the Judaism of Jerusalem; and they had much in common—Samaritan-type Pentateuchs, e.g., have been found at Qumran, and patristic evidence locates a group of Essenes in Samaria. The strong probability is that these anti-Jerusalem sectaries were the descendants of the remanent Israel of the period of the Exile.[5]

The central historical problem—and the solution now commending itself with the discovery of the scrolls—may be stated and formulated, in fairly general terms, along the following lines. One hundred years ago the French liberal theologian Ernst Renan (author of the classic *Vie de Jésus*) declared that "Christianity is an Essenism which has largely succeeded". The theory that it was from this monastic or semi-monastic Essene sect of Jewish ascetics that Christianity sprang became a subject of violent and bitter controversy; and echoes of this controversy have reached our own day. Not the least formidable of the objections to it was that it seemed to place the origins of the Christian Church within the context of a rigidly ascetic type of Judaism. The debate is now itself a subject of historical investigation; and the most recent account of it runs to nearly 300 pages, with a selected bibliography of more than 30 pages.[6] The hub of the problem and the main lines of its solution were put clearly and cogently by two of the leading protagonists in the old liberal controversy, David Friedrich Strauss,[7] on the one side, and Herman Grätz, on the other. Strauss declared in 1872 that the connection of Christian beginnings with Essenism was "an assumption at once as inescapable as it was incapable of demonstration".[8] On the other side, the Jewish historian Grätz maintained vigorously that, on the evidence then known, the assumption of such a historical link was not only inescapable; it was both demonstrable and indeed had been demonstrated. Grätz referred to Jesus as an Essene prophet and to his teaching as Essene teaching. Judgement was, in the main, given for Strauss; and the debate rested till the discovery of the Dead Sea Scrolls.

The identity of the Qumran sectarians with the Essenes is now a widely accepted hypothesis[9] so that we possess in the Dead Sea Scrolls evidence undreamt of at the time of the Essene controversy, and of incalculable value, since it is first-hand evidence, unlike the often garbled and second-hand versions of the facts to be found in patristic sources. The question now becomes: Does this new evidence support the theory that the Essene sect constituted, as it were, the matrix of the primitive Church? Is the Christian Church a child of Essenism?

It would seem that the new evidence requires, in general, an affirmative answer, provided we do not define Essenism too narrowly, for instance, by equating it exclusively with the Dead Sea group, but are prepared to understand the term as a general description of this widespread movement of anti-Jerusalem, anti-Pharisaic non-conformity of the period. It is from such an "Essene-type" of Judaism that Christianity is descended. But while a general historical connection, so defined and understood, may now be certain, we have still to assess the extent of the influence of this non-conformist Essene-type Judaism on Christianity; and, even more important, we have still to form a judgement about what is original, over against what is derivative, in the Christian religion of which Essenism represents, as it were, the larval stage.[10]

There are at least three important common areas of religious and theological thought and practice where historical connection or dependence of emerging Christian ideas on Qumran seems probable. They are (1) the ascetic element in the Qumran and Christian tradition; (2) the doctrine of salvation or soteriology; and (3) Qumran and Christian eschatology—a common doctrine of the *eschata* or Last Things. All of these topics have been touched on or dealt with in the preceding essays. The following reflections contain a selection of additional illustrations of common ground in these three overlapping areas of religion and theology, where the facts are not in dispute, and the resemblances are too close to be coincidental.

1. With regard to the ascetic element in the two traditions, I leave aside here the question with which I have dealt elsewhere, whether we can actually trace Christian monasticism and the ideal of celibacy (or virginity) in the early Church (perpetuated in the Roman Church) to the Essene-type Judaism of Qumran.[11] The answer, it seems to me, must again be an affirmative one, but this does not mean that all the problems are thereby solved. The question, for instance, of the nature of the ideal of celibacy at Qumran is still in many ways an open one.[12] That this was a Qumran ideal and institution I do not doubt, in spite of the paucity of evidence in the Scrolls themselves. I am concerned in this essay solely with the problem of the ascetic element or strain in the New Testament writings themselves, and in its possible derivation from an Essene-type Judaism, such as flourished at Qumran.

John the Baptist was undoubtedly an ascetic, bound by what appears to be a life-long Nazirite vow; he may, indeed, like Samson, have belonged to the class of the life-long Nazirate.[13] Moreover, as Dr Scobie points out,[14] John's asceticism appears to have been even stricter than that practised at Qumran since the Qumran Essenes evidently ate bread and drank wine, possibly a form of lightly fermented "sweet wine", though this is not certain.[15] It seems unlikely that Luke 7. 33 par. is to be taken literally; it is more important for the contrast it points between Jesus and the Baptist, for if the later is unmistakably an ascetic, the former is as undeniably no ascetic, but, certainly in the respects mentioned, a very ordinary son of man.

It is at this point that Grätz's theory that Jesus was an Essene must be seriously challenged since the testimony of Luke 7. 33 par. as an authentic *logion* is fully supported by the Synoptic tradition, which can hardly have been invented, that Jesus of Nazareth associated with "publicans and sinners", a class not given to ascetic ways. Furthermore, there is evidence to show that Jesus could disapprove of the strict rigoristic legalism of the Essenes just as strongly as he condemned the narrow legalism of the Pharisees. The most illuminating example of this is his condemnation, by implication, of one particular Essene Sabbath regulation: their law forbade the removal of any animal which had accidentally stumbled into a pit on the Sabbath (CD xiii. 22-23). The Pharisees allowed this: only the Essenes condemned it. Jesus said to a group of Pharisees:

"Which of you shall have an ass or an ox fallen into a pit,
and will not straightway pull him out on the sabbath day?"
(Luke 14. 5 (AV))

Jesus cited this piece of Pharisaic humanitarian Sabbath Legislation in support of his healing of the dropsical man on the Sabbath. By implication he condemns the more extreme Essene regulation. In matters of the law, and especially Sabbath observance, the Essenes appear to have out-Phariseed the Pharisees.

This seems to add up to the conclusion that the Jesus was not himself an Essene. Furthermore, there does not seem to be any specifically ascetic strain in his own teaching, unless Matthew 19. 12 about disciples turning themselves into "eunuchs" for the kingdom of God[16] or Jesus' extension of the seventh commandment to the lustful glance (Matthew 5. 27) are equated with "asceticism".[17] Such an Essene ascetic outlook, however, is certainly found elsewhere in the New Testament with unmistakable Essene features. As at Qumran *porneia* or sexual impurity is singled out for special condemnation in the New Testament Epistles and Apocalypse.[18] It is certainly an Essene ascetic ideal we find at Revelation 14. 1; there an élite group—the 144,000 followers of the Lamb—are given a place of special honour in the heavenly Jerusalem: they belong to the

Temple choir of the heavenly city, and are allowed to sing a new song before the heavenly throne. They have been brought (we are told), from among men to be the first-fruit of mankind offered to God—and these words give us some idea of the high priority of their ideal in early Essene-Christian circles. "These are men who did not defile themselves with women, for they have kept themselves chaste[19] and they follow the Lamb wherever he goes." (NEB)

2. I turn now to one area of common belief and crystallizing doctrine of very great importance for the New Testament and its Gospel, viz., the Qumran Essene doctrine of grace and salvation, their soteriology.

The claim has been made that the sect held some kind of belief in a messianic atonement—in an atoning messiah— attributing the same kind of soteriological significance to his sufferings and possible death as Christian belief attaches to the death of Christ. The main protagonist of this view is William Brownlee, who has argued that the Servant Songs in II Isaiah (in particular Isaiah 53) were interpreted at Qumran as referring to the vicarious sufferings of the messiah (or one of the messiahs).[20] The sect believed in two messiahs, one the familiar Davidic figure, the other a priestly messiah. It is not clear from Brownlee's argumentation to which of these figures the Servant variants he cites applied; and in none of the passages where either is mentioned elsewhere is there any unambiguous evidence of an atoning messiah. It may well be, as Jean Starcky has claimed, that it was the priestly messiah who was to make atonement as the Servant of the Lord. Driver regards the evidence as too shaky to bear the weight of the theory; and the idea has been vigorously opposed by Milik. Dupont-Sommer found evidence in the *Hodayoth* of the application of the Isaianic prophecies to the Teacher of Righteousness whom he regards as a messianic figure : but this also is questioned. So far as we can be certain, therefore, there is no clear analogy here to Christian belief.[21]

What is clear and certain is that the Suffering Servant Songs, and especially Isaiah 53, are applied to a certain group or council within the sect whose office it is "to make atonement for the land" (Israel) by vicarious suffering. This group or council (*sodh*) was a representative *corps d' élite* in the community.

From the *Damascus Document* and the *War Scroll* we learn that the sect was organized as a military hierocracy, and its organization based on the disposition and mustering of the tribes in the Book of Numbers, chapter 2. At the apex, as it were, was a *corps d'élite* of "twelve men and three priests". Several scholars interpret "twelve men, including three priests" and find in this group a prototype of the Twelve Apostles. But a fragment from Cave 4 spells out the number as "fifteen men". As Milik who drew attention to this, however, points out: "The membership ideally represents the twelve tribes of Israel and the three priestly families descended from Levi through his three sons, Gershon, Kohath, and Merari".[22] We may, in fact, have here the prototype of the College of the Twelve.

The following passage from the *Manual of Discipline* defines their atoning office:

> In the council of the community there shall be twelve men and three priests perfect in all that is revealed from the whole Torah, to act truly, rightly and justly and with a love of mercy; and to walk humbly each with his neighbour; to maintain loyalty in the land, with integrity of purpose and a broken spirit; to expiate wrong-doing as men who uphold the righteous cause [or who act justly] and who endure the afflictions of the refiner's furnace . . .
>
> > For an eternal planting, a Temple for Israel,
> > A conclave which is an holy of holies for Aaron;
> > True witnesses to judgement, and the chosen of grace
> > > to atone for the land.
> > And to render to the wicked their desert.
> > This is the tested wall, the precious corner-stone;
> > Its foundations will not be shaken, nor be removed
> > > from their place.

"True witnesses to judgement": these Qumran saints are to fulfil the mission of the Servant of the Lord (Isaiah 43. 10, 12: "Ye are my witnesses, saith the Lord, and my servant whom I have chosen"), while the "tested wall" and "precious corner-stone" recall Isaiah 28. 16 and 1 Peter 2. 4ff.[23] The most significant words, however, are the description of these Qumran saints as *"true witnesses to judgement, and the chosen of grace to atone for the land"*. Taken in conjunction with an earlier description of the fifteen saints as men who expiate wrongdoing by enduring the afflictions of the refiner's furnace (cf. Daniel 12. 10), we have in these verses the developed theological conception of a community or group within a community identifying itself with the Isaianic Remnant and attributing to its sacrificial sufferings a redemptive function. They are to constitute a living inner sanctuary (a "holy of holies" for Aaron) in the Community, pictured, like the church in the New Testament, as a living Temple, and, like the Son of Man in Daniel, they are to sit in judgement on the wicked.[24]

The Qumran doctrine of grace, along with its closely related doctrine of man—again and again we are reminded of the frailty and inherent sinfulness of man apart from God—is central in Qumran religion. As in the Psalter and the great Prophets, man is always seen in his difference and distance from God but by God's mercy and by his sustaining and enabling power man can transcend his own weakness to become even like one of the heavenly beings themselves. The foundations are here for the Pauline doctrine of "flesh" and "spirit" and "adoption" as "children" or "sons of God" (Rom. 8. 14f).

I QS. xi. 9f. illustrates:

> But as for me, I belong to an evil humanity
> And to the company of wicked flesh.
> My iniquities, my transgressions, my sin . . .
> Belong to the things that move in darkness.
> For a man's way is not his own,
> A man cannot direct his steps (Jeremiah 10. 23)
> But to God belongs rectitude
> And from his hand is integrity of way . . .
> If I stumble, God's mercy is my salvation for ever
> If I stumble in carnal sin, my acquittal [justification] through God's righteousness shall stand everlastingly . . .
> Even from the pit he will draw up my soul, and will direct in the way my steps . . .
> In his mercy he will bring in my acquittal;
> In his steadfast righteousness he will acquit [justify] me . . .

Dr Millar Burrows of Yale has commented on this last verse: "In this verse we seem not only to have justification but sanctification",[25] and he adds, "the point of prime importance here is that while man has no righteousness of his own, there is a righteousness which God, in his own righteousness, freely confers. The meaning of the righteousness of God in Romans 3. 21-26 is thus illustrated and shown to be rooted in pre-Christian Judaism.[26]

This same note of almost "evangelical" piety is struck again and again in the Hymns of Thanksgiving; indeed, one might almost refer to it as a recurring theme. The condemnation of human nature left to its own devices supplies the foil or background to the Qumran doctrine of grace, the mercy and divine strength which God imparts through his enabling spirit. All that is lacking to complete the New Testament doctrine is the Christian belief in the mediation of the Spirit through the Risen and Ascended Lord. It is not too much to claim that, like the Psalmist, these Qumran seers and singers had discovered the open secret of evangelical religion, trust in the mercy of God alone and in his directing spirit to sustain life and conduct. The following from the *Hymns* illustrates perfectly:

I know that righteousness is not in man
Nor perfection of way in the son of man . . .
The way of man cannot be firmly established
Except by the spirit which God has fashioned for him,
To make perfect a way for the sons of men.

[I QH. iv. 27f.]

. . . who is there that is righteous before thee,
When thou bringest him to judgement? . . .
But all the children of thy truth
Thou bringest with forgiveness before thee,
Cleansing them of their transgression by thy great goodness,
And by the multitude of thy mercies making them to stand before
thee for ever.

[I QH. vii. 28f.]

This last verse gives expression to the Qumran belief and hope in
an immortal life and destiny and this is given even fuller expression
in the following lines:

. . . from Sheol . . . thou hast brought me up . . .
And I know that there is hope for him whom thou hast fashioned
   from dust
For the communion of eternity.
The perverse spirit thou hast cleansed from great transgressions
To take its place with the host of the Holy Ones [angels]
And to enter into fellowship with the company of the sons of heaven
For thou hast appointed for man an eternal lot [destiny] . . .

[I QH. iii. 2of.]

Doctrine like this comes very near to that of the New Testament,
in particular Pauline doctrine. Many of the sentiments, of course,
not only anticipate and prepare the way for the New Testament;
they are also a continuation of the piety of the Psalmist or the
religion of the prophets; it is significant, for instance, that Jeremiah
10. 23 ("it is not in man that walketh to direct his steps") supplies
the foundation for the Qumran doctrine. As we move forward, however, to the idea of man's eternal destiny we move more and more
away from the Old Testament until we have practically arrived at
the door of the Gospel.

3. If, one singles out one final general area of doctrine or belief,
in process of crystallizing, as it were, in the Qumran writings and
the New Testament, it would be in their common philosophies of
history, or, more correctly—since both groups of writings assume
that ordinary history is soon to come to an abysmal end—their
doctrine of the Last Things, their "transcendentalizing" Eschatology.
   The idea that not only the human drama but the entire created

universe was played out and playing itself out, was a commonplace of Jewish belief in this period, shared by Pharisees and Essenes alike. This approaching universal crisis or climax of creation is sometimes —somewhat naively—equated with the End of the World. Certainly the belief assumes the end of an old world, the present evil age, to be superseded by a new world, but, in this period where belief and doctrine are still fluid, it is impossible to define exactly what the "End" was expected to be; in fact its shapes and forms are many and varied. Only among the Essenes did it crystallize finally into a single concrete item of belief: just as the first Judgement and destruction of the world under Noah had been by water, now the Last Judgement would be by fire.[27]

The myth is Babylonian in origin. It is said to stem from the Babylonian doctrine of the Great Year, according to which a flood or a conflagration takes place periodically on earth when the planets assume a certain order.[28] It appears in the apocalyptic *Life of Adam and Eve* (xlix. 2)[29] where there is no doubt that it is an Essene doctrine. Its best'known expression occurs in the Essene *Sibylline Oracles* III. 81-87,[30] ". . . then the elements of the world one and all shall be widowed, what time God whose dwelling is in the sky shall roll up the heaven as a book is rolled. And the whole firmament in its varied forms shall fall on the divine earth and on the sea: and then shall flow a ceaseless cataract of raging fire, and shall burn land and sea, and the firmament of heaven and the stars and creation itself it shall cast into one molten mass and clean dissolve."

The final section of one of the most graphic of the Qumran *Hymns of Thanksgiving* gives us what looks like a picture of the Doomsday of the world. Whether the vivid apocalyptic imagery is to be taken literally or figuratively is disputed, but no one doubts that it is eschatological prophecy.[31] The End will be a terrible cataclysm where torrents of fire will destroy all life on earth and the material world will dissolve while the armies of heaven complete the work of destruction. The picture in the writer's mind seems to be that of a universal conflagration accompanying or following Armageddon.

Here we have an undoubted point of contact with the New Testament, especially 2 Peter 3. 5-7: ". . . by water that first world was destroyed, the water of the deluge. And the present heavens and earth, again by God's word, have been kept in store for burning; they are being reserved for the day of judgement when the godless will be destroyed." (NEB)

The nature of the after-life is given distinctive expression in the scrolls by the idea that the loyal covenanters, after the Last Judgement, will enjoy some kind of angelic existence. They are not only to live like angels and consort with angels but to become as angels. In that case, the sect's doctrine of immortality is very similar to that of Luke 20. 35ff., where, in the world to come, men and women are said by Christ to be like the angels or to live as the angels.[32]

It is surprising that no unambiguously clear evidence has so far been produced for any belief by the Qumran sect in the resurrection or in resurrection. Indeed a number of passages appear to imply the old Biblical idea of *she'ol* though in several cases that idea has been developed to become a doctrine of eternal punishment and the fire of the dark regions, that is to say, Gehenna, corresponding to the everlasting or eternal life of the covenanters who escape the wrath of God at the Last Judgement.[33] It would be surprising, however, if the sect had no resurrection doctrine, especially in view of the prominence of the Book of Daniel in their ideas about the Last Judgement. Perhaps some unambiguous evidence may yet be produced to settle this debated point.[34]

It has only been possible, in this essay, to draw attention to these three main aspects of the subject; there are many details to be added and gaps to be filled in. But the relevance and significance of the scrolls for the thought as well as the history of the early Church is beyond doubt. Professor D. E. Nineham has reminded us that one of the few approaches left to us to the complex problem of Christian beginnings is to seek "to wring truth relevant to the history of Jesus from the increasing stock of the remains of the Judaism of his time".[35] That stock has been immensely enriched by the discovery of the scrolls. Moreover, there seems little doubt that the case has been made out that it is from this side of Judaism—an Essene-type Judaism—that Christianity sprang. As Wilcox has argued, there is quite strong evidence at times for some kind of direct historical link between Qumran (or its thought-world) and emerging Christianity. Direct dependence, however, has nowhere been conclusively demonstrated: what we encounter is a stream of common (mainly Old Testament-inspired) tradition and interpretation—a common midrashic source—with, nevertheless, at the same time, yawning chasms of difference and contradiction.[36] Renan was no doubt right: Christianity was an Essenism which succeeded, albeit a Essenism profoundly transformed and transcended by the originality not only of the Apostle to the Gentiles but, at its source, by the mind first of the Baptist and supremely of Jesus of Nazareth; in the last analysis it is (in Driver's words) "the person and position of Christ which make the ultimate difference between the Gospel and the Scrolls".[37]

NOTES

CHAPTER 1

[1] For a tentative chart of Essene chronology see the end of this chapter, which was drawn up after reading H. H. Rowley's "The History of the Qumran Sect" (*Bulletin of the John Rylands Library*, 49 [1966], 203-232). Our dates are about a generation lower for the beginnings of the sect than Rowley's and probably two generations above the dates of A. Dupont-Sommer (who has been increasingly cautious in proposing any dates).

[2] On the text see the critical edition by D. Detlefsen, *Die geographischen Bücher . . . der Naturalis Historia* [Berlin, 1904], p. 104 (on the first line of v, 73). Note that *litore* is a variant of *litora* and that two lines below the same MS offers *eoque* instead of *ex aequo*.

[3] See the expedition report (published under the unfortunate title *Search for Sodom and Gomorrah* (Kansas City, Mo., 1962), pp. 154-189, with an analysis of laboratory tests by Dr K. O. Emery, pp. 305-320.

[4] See especially his Schweich Lectures: *L'archéologie et les manuscrits de la Mer Morte* (London, 1961), and his trenchant reply to G. R. Driver (see below, § IV) in *Rev. Bib.*, 73 (1966), 212-235, and in condensed translation, *New Blackfriars*, May 1966, 396-410. We have not intentionally deviated anywhere from de Vaux's archaeological analysis, which seems eminently reasonable throughout.

[5] See especially Paul W. Lapp, *Palestinian Ceramic Chronology 200 B.C.-A.D. 70* (New Haven, American Schools of Oriental Research, 1961).

[6] See *Jour. Bib. Lit.*, 56 (1937), 145-176; *Bull. Amer. Sch. Or. Res.*, No. 110 (1948), 3 (preferring a date in the second century B.C. for I QSIs^a whereas in his original letter to John C. Trever (March 15, 1948) one of the writers had suggested a date "around 100 B.C." (*The Biblical Archaeologist*, 11, No. 3 (1948), 55). On the picture as it had emerged a decade later see the basic study by Frank M. Cross, Jr, in *The Bible and the Ancient Near East* (ed. G. Ernest Wright, New York, 1961), 133-202. Since then the discoveries at Wâdi Dâliyeh and Masada (see below) have established palaeographic chronology for the entire period represented at Qumran.

[7] See now J. Liver, *Revue de Qumran*, 6 (1967), 3-30.

[8] It is, however, increasingly probable that the order of high priests preserved by Josephus is correct after all, and that Ecclesiasticus was composed well before the end of the third century, since the Jewish historian (who is by far our earliest source) clearly dated Simon the Just in the time of Philadelphus (285-247 B.C.).

[9] There is a close relation in some respects between the *Hôdayôt*, which we should date in the time of the *Ḥasîdîm* (*Asidaioi*), roughly between 175 and 160 B.C., and the second part of Enoch, undoubtedly composed in Hebrew (the "Discourses," Enoch 37-71), as we hope to show elsewhere. The fact that no fragments of this part of Enoch have yet been found at Qumran proves nothing about the date of composition.

[10] See L. Finkelstein, *Harvard Theological Review*, 36 (1943), 19-24, followed by E. Bickerman (e.g., *The Jews*, ed. Finkelstein, I, 112, n.52) and Albright (*From the Stone Age to Christianity*, 1957 ed., 20).

[11] See the treatment by E. Bickerman, *Jour. Bib. Lit.*, 69 (1950), 245-260, who convincingly dates the original Testaments in the first quarter of the second century or the last decades of the third century B.C.

[12] There is every reason to accept the now usual etymology of Greek *Essaioi* or *Essēnoi* as derived from Aramaic and Syriac *ḥasyâ*, "pious, holy," or rather from the plural **ḥassayyâ* > **ḥassayyâ* > **ḥassê*. Note that *ḥet* followed by *ă* in a syllable closed by non-velarized consonants, appears in Hellenistic-Roman Greek transcriptions as *epsilon* (e.g., *Ḥammôt* becomes as a rule *Emmaous*). Note also that Philo renders "Essene" by Greek *hosios*, and that the latter word is translated in Syriac as *ḥasyâ* (Acts 2. 27). Since the word *ḥasîd* seems never to occur in the hitherto published Qumran literature, it would appear that it was avoided by the Essenes themselves, and that its Aramaic equivalent was applied to them by pagan and non-Essene Jewish speakers of Aramaic. This linguistic divergence would then be a drastic example of the growing break between the pious followers of the early Maccabees and the Essene sect as such.

[13] The date is established by cuneiform documents. The occupation of Babylonia was accompanied and followed by a widespread break-down of political organization, and the two great rivers of Babylonia were allowed to burst through their dykes (levees), thus putting an end for generations to prosperous agricultural life south of Babylon. For instance, the famous city of Orchoe (Erech), on the ancient course of the Euphrates, had to be abandoned in the year 139 B.C. On the Babylonian origin of the Essenes see the discussion by Albright in *From the Stone Age to Christianity* (1940 ed.), 298 ff., which has been con-firmed throughout by the Qumran documents, as far as they go; on this see Mann in *The Anchor Bible: Acts* (1967), 281 f.

[14] This is the only correct translation, since both the verb and the noun are used with *derekh*, "way", in biblical, post-biblical, and modern Hebrew, and the opposite term, *môreh sheqer*, means "false guide" in the Bible. Besides in the passage we have cited in CD i. 9 ff. the members of the earlier group are said to have been "blind and groping for the way (*derek*) before the *môreh ṣedeq* appeared.

[15] On Simon Maccabaeus as the Wicked Priest see the convincing demonstration by Frank M. Cross, Jr in *The Ancient Library of Qumran and Modern Biblical Studies* (1958), 101-117.

[16] Dr Samuel Iwry first called attention to the passages CD viii. 23f. and 36 f. (A. M. Habermann, *Megilloth Midbar Yehuda*, 1959, p. 82),

which prove that the Right Guide was believed by his immediate followers to have died a natural death.

[17] That the War Scroll is not strictly Essene follows from such details as mention of the traditional Jewish name of the angel Michael (which does not occur in original Essene literature, including the angelology published by J. Strugnell) and especially from the absence of so much that is characteristically Essene. If we follow the plausible dating of Y. Yadin in the second half of the first century B.C., the War Scroll would seem to be intermediate between classical Essene writings composed between c. 140 and 50 B.C. and the rise of the Zealots after A.D. 6. In other words, its author may have been an Essene who had moved close to the position later taken by the Zealots. To this extent G. R. Driver and Cecil Roth seem to be on the right track.

[18] See the references given at the end of n. 13, above.

[19] See n. 12, above.

[20] Extensive new cuneiform material has been published by W. G. Lambert and A. R. Millard, *Cuneiform Texts . . . from the British Museum*, XLVI (1965), Nos. 1-15, and a complete re-editing and new translation will appear soon.

[21] For the present see the epoch-making analysis of Acts 7 by Spiro (edited by Albright and Mann) in the Anchor *Acts* (1967), 285-300.

CHAPTER 2

[1] Cf. E. F. Sutcliffe, *The Monks of Qumran* (1960), pp. xi, 152 f.; A. R. C. Leaney, *The Rule of Qumran and Its Meaning* (1966), pp. 210 f.

[2] A. Dupont-Sommer, *The Jewish Sect of Qumran and the Essenes* (1956), p. 87.

[3] G. Vermes, *Discovery in the Judaean Desert* (1956), p. 17.

[4] F. F. Bruce, *Second Thoughts on the Dead Sea Scrolls* (1961), p. 117.

[5] W. H. Brownlee, *The Biblical Archaeologist* (1951), XIV, No. 3, p. 54.

[6] J. M. Allegro, *The Dead Sea Scrolls* (1956), p. 90.

[7] Cf. F. M. Cross, *The Ancient Library of Qumran and Modern Biblical Studies* (1961), p. 68.

[8] C. H. H. Scobie, *John the Baptist* (1964), p.93.

[9] Cf. R. K. Harrison, *The Archeology of the Old Testament* (1963), pp. 109 ff.

[10] Cf. S. Talmon, *Scripta Hierosolymitana* (1957), IV, pp. 162 seq.

CHAPTER 3

[1] The innumerable theories are summarized in M. Burrows, *The Dead Sea Scrolls* and *More Light on the Dead Sea Scrolls* (New York: Viking, 1955, 1958). While the theory we propose above has solid scholarly support, it is far from unanimously accepted. In particular, some would date the Teacher to the Roman period in the first century B.C./A.D. The best works are G. Jeremias, *Der Lehrer der Gerechtigkeit* (Göttingen: Mohr, 1963) and J. Carmignac, *Christ and the Teacher of Righteousness* (Baltimore: Helicon, 1962). G. R. Driver's theories on *The Judaean Scrolls* (Blackwell, Oxford, 1965) are the most recent additions to this controversial subject.

[2] CD i. 5-8 puts 390 years between the fall of Jerusalem to Nebuchadnezzar (587 B.C.) and the time when God caused a new planting to grow forth from Israel. If we recognize that Jewish estimates of the post-exilic period are often short by twenty or thirty years, this information brings us close to 167 B.C. The author of IV QpNah. speaks of a period "from the time of Antiochus until the coming of the rulers of the Kittim" (i.e., the Romans)—probably the span of the sect's existence until the moment in the Roman period when the author is writing.

[3] The genitive probably has a double meaning: what he teaches constitutes a way of righteousness, and he himself is righteous. M. Black, *The Dead Sea Scrolls and Christian Doctrine* (University of London, 1966) p. 8, makes the interesting suggestion that "righteous" is equivalent to "rightful, legitimate" and that since teaching the Law was the chief function of the high-priestly office, the title "Righteous Teacher" was given in recognition that he was the rightful high priest.

[4] This dating is explained by the fact that Qumran followed its own calendar; indeed seemingly one of the factors in the dispute between Qumran and the Jerusalem priests was the abandoning of the ancient solar calendar in Jerusalem worship. The day described may have been a holy day for the Teacher but not for the Priest, for the violation of a high holy day by the Maccabean high priest would have shocked all.

[5] For this reconstruction of the text see P. Skehan, *Catholic Biblical Quarterly* XXI (1959), p. 75.

[6] G. Jeremias, op. cit., attributes to him at least these hymns: ii. 1-19; ii. 31-39; iii. 1-18; iv. 5—v. 4; v. 5-19; v. 20—vii. 5; vii. 6-25; viii. 4-40.

[7] Not every reference to the Interpreter of the Law is necessarily a reference to the Teacher, for certainly the function of interpreting the Law had to go on in the community after the Teacher's death. Some scholars have even proposed that there was also a functionary named the Teacher of Righteousness throughout the community's existence after the death of the original Teacher. Black (op. cit., p. 9) thinks of two Righteous Teachers, the founder of the sect in the second century B.C. and a later teacher in the first century B.C.

[8] This is said in commentary on the famous Hab. 2. 4b: "The righteous man shall live by his faith". However, faith in the Teacher is not the same as the faith in Christ of which Paul speaks; it is primarily faith in the Teacher's correctness and authority as an interpreter of the Law.

[9] CD xix. 35 speaks of "the gathering in of the Teacher"; the same term is used in Gen. 25. 8, 17; 35. 29; 49. 29, 33 to describe the peaceful death of the patriarchs and their reunion with their ancestors in the family tomb. It militates against the thesis that the Teacher was put to death by enemies.

[10] We are discussing, then, Messiah(s) with a capital M. This does not mean we are imposing any Christian connotations on the word, for the Qumran expectation lies completely within the scope of Judaism and reflects none of the reinterpretation of the concept of Messiah

necessitated by the identification of Jesus as the Messiah. But neither are we speaking of a vague class of those anointed (i.e., chosen) by God. CD ii. 12 exhibits the latter usage when it describes the prophets as those "anointed with His holy spirit".

[11] We omit reference to IV Q Test, sometimes referred to as "a collection of messianic proof-texts" (Vermes). The identification of the texts cited in this document so that they refer to the prophet and the two Messiahs (I QS. ix. 11) is most dubious. The first text is not Deut. 5. 28-9 but Exod. 20. 21 according to a proto-Samaritan text tradition. The Star of Num. 24. 15-17 referred to in the second text is for Qumran a priestly, not a Davidic, figure. We omit reference to the Aramaic "Elect of God" text (IV Q Mess. ar). Its editor, J. Starcky, thought that it dealt with the birth and growth of the Messiah, but J. A. Fitzmyer, *Catholic Biblical Quarterly* XXVII (1965) 348-72, has shown that it probably refers to Noah or some other figure of the past. We omit reference to the Melchizedek text of Cave 11. Line 18 is a pesher interpretation of "the bringer of good tidings" in Isa. 52. 7. The editor, A. S. van der Woude, originally thought it to read that the bringer is the Messiah; but Y. Yadin, *Israel Exploration Journal* XV (1965) 152-54, has shown that more likely it states that the bringer is one anointed with the Spirit. (This may still be messianic, but the meaning is not clear.) Finally we omit all discussion of I QH iii. 3-18, the so-called Messianic Psalm or Hymn, which describes a woman giving birth, in imagery taken from Isa. 9. 6. What this hymn is all about remains a mystery.

[12] The prophet mentioned may be Elijah; but since laws are mentioned in the context, the reference is probably to the Prophet like Moses of Deut. 18. 18. Actually both Elijah and the Prophet like Moses figured in Qumran thought. The suggestion that the Messiah of Aaron is Elijah should be rejected, even though Elijah became a messianic figure in later Israel. He was certainly not a Zadokite priest, and Qumran would never have dreamed of a supreme Priest who was not Zadokite.

[13] The context in I QSb. v. 20-7 draws heavily from Isa. 11. 1-5; IV QpIs[a] ii. 21-28 applies this text of Isaiah to the "Branch of David who shall arise at the end".

[14] The basic chronological outline of Qumran messianic development has been supplied by J. Starcky, *Revue Biblique* LXX (1963) 481-505. He puts CD in the period 63-37 B.C. For objections to this and for grammatical possibilities of the CD references to the Messiah(s) see R. E. Brown, *Catholic Biblical Quarterly* XXVIII (1966) 51-57. There are important scholars who do not believe that Qumran expected a Messiah Priest; for example, A. J. B. Higgins, N.T.S. VIII (1967) 211-39, thinks of one (Davidic) Messiah representing the two branches of the community, Aaron and Israel.

[15] It is debated whether the *Testaments* is a Jewish work with Christian interpolations or a Christian work drawing on Jewish sources. There is proto-testamental literature at Qumran. For the two Messiahs in the *Testaments* see G. R. Beasley-Murray, *JTS* XLVIII (1947) 1-17.

[16] Apparently a medieval discovery of Qumran documents near Jericho influenced Karaite thinkers. For the messianism of the Karaites see N. Wieder, *Journal of Semitic Studies* VI (1955) 14-25.

CHAPTER 4

[1] Never the "last things" in the D.S.S. but the "end of days", or "coming days"; CD iv. 4; vi. 11. I QS. i. I.E.; I QpHab. ii. 5-6, ix. 6 *passim.*

[2] S. Mowinckel, *He that Cometh* (Oxford 1956), trans. G. W. Anderson, *Han Som Kommer*, Copenhagen, 1951, pp. 125-6.

[3] S. Mowinckel, *He that Cometh*, op. cit., p. 419.

[4] T. C. Vriezen, "Prophecy and Eschatology", *Vetus Testamentum*, Suppl. I (Leiden 1953), pp. 199-229.

[5] iii. 22-23. J. Pryke, " 'Spirit' and 'Flesh' in the Qumran Documents and some New Testament Texts", *Revue de Qumran*, 19 November, 1965, pp. 345-360 (full Bibliography at the end of this article).

[6] Isa. 9. 6. quoted in part in iii. 10; M. Black, *The Scrolls and Christian Origins*, Edinburgh, 1961, pp. 149 ff. G. Hinson, "Hodayoth III, 6-18, In What Sense Messianic?", *Revue de Qumran*, VI, February 1960, pp. 183-204.

[7] *yolidh* or *yolikh*; probably the former, D. Barthélemy and J. T. Milik, *Discoveries in the Judaean Desert I, Qumran Cave I* (Oxford 1955), p. 117.

[8] CD xx. 10-12 and J. Carmignac, "Le Retour du Docteur de Justice à la fin des Jours?", *Revue de Qumran*, 2 Oct. 1958, pp. 235-248; M. Mansoor, *The Dead Sea Scrolls* (Leiden, 1961), pp. 157, 161. W. H. Brownlee, *The Meaning of the Qumran Scrolls for the Bible*, (Oxford, 1964), pp. 133, 149, 151 (n. 63).

[9] R. B. Laurin, "The Question of Immortality in the Qumran Hodayot", *Journal of Semitic Studies*, III, Oct. 1958, pp. 344-355; J. van der Ploeg, "L'immortalité de l'homme d'après les textes de la Mer Morte", *Vetus Testamentum*, II, 1952, pp. 171-175; C. Rabin, *Qumran Studies*, (Oxford, 1957), pp. 73-74.

[10] M. Black, "The Account of the Essenes in Hippolytus and Josephus", *The Background of the New Testament and Its Eschatology*, W. D. Davies and D. Daube, (Cambridge, 1956), p.175.

[11] M. Delcor, "Recherches sur un horoscope en langue hébraique provenant de Qumran", *Revue de Qumran*, 20 July, 1966, pp. 521-542; J. Carmignac, "Les Horoscopes de Qumran", *Revue de Qumran*, 18 April 1965, pp. 199-217.

[12] A full bibliography can be found in the following: E. J. Pryke, "Some Aspects of Eschatology in the Dead Sea Scrolls" *Studia Evangelica*, vol. V, ed. F. L. Cross, pp. 296-302 (*Texte und Untersuchungen zur Geschichte der altchristlichen Literatur*, Akademie-Verlag, Berlin, 1968).

CHAPTER 5

[1] Works on John the Baptist written before the Dead Sea Scrolls were available include M. Goguel, *Au Seuil De l'Evangile: Jean-Baptiste*, Payot, 1928; C. H. Kraeling, *John the Baptist*, Scribner's 1951. For

studies since the Scrolls see W. H. Brownlee, "John the Baptist in the New Light of Ancient Scrolls", in K. Stendahl, *The Scrolls and the New Testament*, Harper, 1957, pp. 33-53; C. H. H. Scobie, *John the Baptist*, S.C.M., 1964. A penetrating study and interpretation of "John the Baptist in the Gospel Tradition" by W. Wink is appearing as No. 7 in the Monograph Series of *Studiorum Novi Testamenti Societas*, Cambridge, 1968.

[2] I QH iii. 27-32. Translation from T. H. Gaster, *The Scriptures of the Dead Sea Sect*, Secker and Warburg, 1957, pp. 142, 143.

[3] Cf. R. K. Harrison, Essay in *The Rites and Customs of the Qumran Sect*, pp. 7, 8.

[4] See C. H. Dodd, *Historical Tradition in the Fourth Gospel*, Cambridge, 1963, pp. 280, 281.

[5] See J. T. Milik, *Ten Years of Discovery in the Wilderness of Judaea*, S.C.M., 1959, p. 105; A. R. C. Leaney, *The Rule of Qumran and its Meaning*, S.C.M., 1966, p. 184.

[6] Cf. R. Bultmann, *The History of the Synoptic Tradition*, Blackwell, 1963, p. 246; U. W. Mauser, *Christ in the Wilderness*, S.C.M., 1963, p.75.

[7] See C. H. Dodd, op. cit., p. 253.

CHAPTER 7

[1] E.g., CD xi. 13 ff., where it is forbidden to help deliver a labouring animal on the Sabbath, or even to rescue her new-born young from a cistern or pit, if she happens to have let it fall into one. The Sabbath must be kept.

[2] E.g., Psalms 22, 42, 44, etc.

[3] Daniel 11. 33, 35, 12. 3, 10.

[4] Cf. also IV QSl. 39 and IV QSl. 40, and J. Strugnell, "The Angelic liturgy at Qumrân, 4Q Serek Šîrôt Ôlat Haššabāt", *Supplements to Vetus Testamentum*, Vol. VII, Leiden, 1960, pp. 318-45, esp. p. 320.

[5] I QS. iv. 22.

[6] I QS. iv. 22.

[7] E.g., T. Asher i. 3-9, T. Judah xx. 1.

[8] K. G. Kuhn, A. Dupont-Sommer, and others.

[9] Yasna xxx, 3 ff.

[10] "New Light on Temptation, Sin, and Flesh in the New Testament", in *The Scrolls and the New Testament*, Ed. K. Stendahl, New York (1957), pp. 94-113; here, p. 98.

[11] b. Sukk. 52a. The matter is discussed in detail in St.-B. IV, 482-83.

[12] Cf. CD vi. 13, vii. 19-20, IV Q Test. 9ff., etc.

[13] B. Reicke, "Traces of Gnosticism in the Dead Sea Scrolls?" *NTS* I (1954-55), 137-141; p. 140. Cf. W. H. Brownlee, "The Dead Sea Manual of Discipline", *BASOR Supplemental Studies*, 10-12, New Haven, 1951, p. 45, n. 25.

[14] loc. cit.

[15] Isa. 40. 13, etc

[16] See the discussion of this passage in G. Bornkamm, *GesAufs* I, München 1963, pp. 70-5.

17 *Kultzeiten und kultischer Bundesschluss in der "Ordensregeal" vom Toten Meer*, Leiden (1961), p. 91. (translation mine).
18 op. cit., p. 93 (translation mine).
19 Weise, op. cit., pp. 89 ff.
20 " 'Knowledge' in the Dead Sea Scrolls and in Matthew 11 : 25-30", *HTR* xlvi (1953), pp. 113-39, especially p. 120.
21 *The Temple and the Community in Qumran and the New Testament*, SNTS Monograph Series I, Cambridge (1965), pp. 49 ff.
22 Cf. the more detailed discussion in the writer's *The Semitisms of Acts*, Oxford (1965), pp. 35-37; esp. p. 37.
23 op. cit., pp. 96-8, 98, n. 1.
24 Kuhn, loc. cit., pp. 101, 107.
25 "Paul and The Dead Sea Scrolls: Flesh and Spirit", in *The Scrolls and the New Testament*, pp. 157-82; p. 171.

CHAPTER 8

1 BASOR, Supplementary Studies, Nos. 10–12 (1951), p. 58.
2 *The Jewish Sect of Qumran and the Essenes*, p. 152.
3. *Scrolls from the Wilderness of the Dead Sea* (University of California, 1965), p. 12.
4 Cf. above, pp. 81, 96.
5 See my *Scrolls*, p. 61ff.
6 Siegfried Wagner, *Die Essener in der wissensch. Diskussion, Beihefte zur Z.A.W.*, 79 (Berlin, 1960).
7 Author of the famous *Leben Jesu*, translated into English by George Eliot.
8 "Auch in die Anfänge des Christenthums, dessen Zusammenhang mit dem Essenismus, eine eben so unabweisliche wie unerweisliche Voraussetzung bleibt, sehen wir diese Richtung [der Essäer] hineinspielen." *Der alte und der neue Glaube* (Leipzig, 1872), p. 252.
9 See above, p. 11 ff.
10 Cf. Renan's remark: "Essenism, which seems to have been directly related to the apocalyptic school, originated about the same time, and offered as it were a first rough sketch of the great discipline soon to be instituted for the education of mankind." (Translation according to Dupont Sommer, *The Essene Writings from Qumran* (Blackwell, 1961), p. 369.) English edn. The Scott Library, *Life of Jesus*, p. 11.
A possible historical link between this widespread movement of anti-Pharisaic non-conformity (an "Essene-type Judaism") and Christianity may not have been "the sect of the Nazarenes" (Acts 24. 5, 14), if this was, in fact, as Epiphanius (fourth century) claims, a pre-Christian and north-Palestinian Jewish "sect", located in the Mount Hermon area. See my *Scrolls and Christian Origins*, pp. 66ff. For an admirable discussion of "Jewish Christianity in Acts in the light of the Qumran Scrolls", see J. A. Fitzmyer in *Studies in Luke-Acts* (essays presented in honour of Paul Schubert) ed. by L. E. Keck and J. L. Martyn (S.P.C.K., 1968), pp. 233ff.

[11] *Scrolls*, pp. 45, 83ff. "The Tradition of Hasidean-Essene Asceticism: Its Origins and Influence", in *Aspects du Judéo-Christianisme* (Paris, 1965), pp. 29ff.

[12] See my Dr Williams' Lecture on *The Essene Problem* (London, 1961), pp. 13ff.

[13] See my *Scrolls*, p. 167.

[14] Above, p. 66.

[15] Ibid., loc. cit.

[16] Matthew 19. 12 is the scriptural and dominical foundation for the institution of monasticism or a celibate clergy. It is questionable, however, whether Jesus intended this form of self-dedication to become institutionalized, as it was in Essenism and is still in the Roman tradition.

[17] Cf., however, J. Allegro, *The Dead Sea Scrolls: A reappraisal*, p. 114, on Mark 5. 27–28, and D. F. Strauss, op. cit., p. 253.

[18] See *The Essene Problem*, pp. 14ff.

[19] Literally "These (ones) are *parthenoi* (virgins)". For the special use of this word in the New Testament and patristic writings, see my *Scrolls*, pp. 83ff.

[20] *The Meaning of the Qumran Scrolls for the Bible, with special attention to the Book of Isaiah* (New York, O.U.P., 1964).

[21] Did the sect believe that their Messiah(s) would rise again from the dead? Mr Pryke (p. 54 above) hints at such a possibility suggested by one interpretation of CD vi. 11. A useful review of the literature on this ambiguous verse is given by G. Jeremias in his *Der Lehrer der Gerechtigkeit* (Göttingen, 1963), pp. 284ff. I have discussed the verse fully in my Ethel M. Wood Lecture on *The Dead Sea Scrolls and Christian Doctrine* (London, 1966), pp. 10ff. In that lecture I pointed out that *moreh haṣṣedek*, Rightful Teacher (rather than Teacher of Righteousness) was a title for the legitimate or rightful High Priest whom the sect expected "to arise", i.e. "to appear", "come forward" "at the end of the days", the latter phrase originally referring to the end of the forty-year period of the sect's wilderness wanderings. It is bad theology based on superficial semantics which interprets this to mean the return to life or "resurrection" of the founder of the sect, i.e., its first Rightful Teacher or messianic pretender to high-priestly office. It is thoroughly bad philology to translate "arise" by "resurrection": if the word here means anything more than "arise" it means "until the *appointment* of the latter-day Rightful Teacher". It is precisely the same formula as is used several times for the "coming" ((or appointment) of the Messiah of Aaron and Israel, the same individual, the latter-day Rightful Teacher or High Priest of the sect who will exercise the same priestly functions as lawgiver as the priestly founder of the Community. Cf. p. 40 above.

[22] *Ten Years of Discovery in the Wilderness of Judea* (S.C.M., 1959), p. 100. Cf. also F. F. Bruce, above, pp. 75ff.

[23] The parallels have been worked out in detail by Bertil Gärtner in his study *The Temple and the Community in Qumran and the New Testament*, SNTS Monograph Series, No. 1, Cambridge, 1965.

[24] Cf. above, p. 75.

25 BASOR, Supp. Stud., 10-12 (1951), p. 45.

26 *The Dead Sea Scrolls*, p. 334.

27 *Scrolls and Christian Origins*, p. 142. Cf. Pryke, above, p. 54 ff.

28 The doctrine is said to have been made known in the West by a Babylonian priest Berogus, mentioned by Josephus and, in this connection by Seneca, *Quaest*, nat. 3. 29, Cf. E. M. Sidebottom, *James, Jude, and 2 Peter* (Century Bible), pp. 119ff.

29 Adam is told: "Our Lord will bring upon your race the anger of his judgement, first by water, the second time by fire; by these two will the Lord judge the whole human race" (Charles, *Apocrypha and Pseudepigrapha of the Old Testament*, p. 152).

30 Ed. Charles, op. cit.

31 *Scrolls and Christian Origins*, pp. 137ff. Cf. above, Pryke, p. 54.

32 *Scrolls and Christian Origins*, pp. 141ff. But cf. above, p. 88.

33 *Scrolls and Christian Origins*, pp. 138ff.

34 *Scrolls and Christian Origins*, pp. 141ff. Milik has suggested that the north-south orientation of the graves at Qumran, with the head at the south end, was dictated by the wish that at the general resurrection the pious covenanter would raise to gaze on the paradise of God which the Essenes located in the north. Cf. P. Grelot, "La Géographie mythique d'Henoch et ses sources orientales", and J. T. Milik, "Henoch au pays des aromates", in *Revue Biblique*, tom. 65 (1958), pp. 33ff, 70ff; *Scrolls*, p. 140.

35 *Journal of Theological Studies* (1960), pp. 260ff.

36 Wilcox p. 96; Bruce, pp. 72ff.

37 *The Judaean Scrolls*, p. 548.

INDEX OF AUTHORS

8

INDEX OF SUBJECTS

INDEX OF
BIBLICAL REFERENCES

INDEX OF
QUMRAN REFERENCES

INDEX OF REFERENCES
TO APOCRYPHA AND PSEUDEPIGRAPHA